Collection Management:
Current Issues

Edited by Sarah Shoemaker

NEAL-SCHUMAN PUBLISHERS, INC.
New York, London   1989

Published by Neal-Schuman Publishers, Inc.
23 Leonard Street
New York, NY 10013

Copyright © 1989 by Neal-Schuman Publishers, Inc.

Printed and bound in the United States of America

Library of Congress Cataloging-in-Publication Data

Collection management.
   Includes index.
   1. Collection development (Libraries)
I. Shoemaker, Sarah.
Z687.C66   1989   025.2'1   89-3258
ISBN 1-55570-034-9

Contents

Foreword

Collection Management: Current Issues honors a librarian whose career spanned forty years at the University of Michigan, during which time she witnessed and helped to shape incredible changes in the field of collection development. To pay her proper tribute, one must appreciate fully the magnitude of the changes and the various configurations of collection development she faced during her tenure.

This book deals with collection management issues that currently confront university libraries and their users. My task is to share with the reader the way it was around 1945, when Mona East was appointed by the University of Michigan Library as a junior order librarian.

Throughout the period following World War II bibliographers such as Felix Reichmann of Cornell, and R.C. Stewart of Michigan, played dominant roles in the building of collections and working with faculty. This was also a time when academic libraries were struggling to shift from faculty-dominated selection to greater participation by librarian bibliographers. As late as 1957, Harry Bach surveyed fifty-four academic libraries and found that in the majority "materials are selected by the faculty with the aid and advice of the library. . . . The librarian and library staff supplement and round out faculty buying in the various fields and select those works which are not specifically needed for the work of particular departments. They also call faculty members' attention to important publications in their field." On the other hand "libraries in which materials are selected by the library with the aid and advice of the faculty . . . represent . . . the avant guard of librarianship in the matter of library responsibility in book selection. . . . At Columbia, for instance, . . . supervising librarians and department heads do the day-to-day selecting of publications for the collections under their immediate control. Although faculty members make recommendations as to items to be purchased, the library relies upon its staff members to

. . . indicate significant publications which shall be acquired."

In the fifties, as book budgets increased, more and more responsibility for book selection was transferred into the hands of library bibliographers. They became the institutional memories because they operated with such a broad perspective. A person like Mona East carries years of knowledge about her own university's collection and that memory can never be replicated or repeated.

With the increased use of approval plans, the growth in the quantity of scholarly publications, the increased role of staff in governance, the more accepted view that selection is a part of the librarian's professional responsibility, and the increased use of subject specialists on staff, the bibliographer is gradually giving way to collection development specialists. Now we use terms such as "management" and "coordination" which embrace traditional development activities. Looking at collection development only in terms of ordering books has given way to a whole new definition of "collection management." The contemporary collection manager must be concerned with new technologies, preservation, budgeting, evaluation of the collection, shared collection development, space/storage issues, and management issues.

Mona East served as a link between the bibliographical traditions of her predecessors and the current pattern in which dozens of professionals actively engage in collection development. Responsibility for creating a decentralized "selection infrastructure" at Michigan fell to Mona during a very turbulent period. New scientific and technical sub-disciplines sprang up almost overnight; fluctuations in currencies and economic inflation diminished the purchasing power of the library's book budget. Funds were often tight and difficult choices had to be made, but these choices were always made wisely.

One of Mona's primary objectives was to preserve the traditional strengths of the libraries' broad collections, and at the same time achieve a reasonable balance between extensive humanities and social sciences collections housed in the Graduate Library against the division (branch) libraries in which reside most of the science and technology collections. Often Mona was forced to walk a tightrope without the aid of a balance pole. And while frictions occasionally occurred everyone understood Mona's purpose and appreciated her fairness. In retrospect, I think her efforts were very successful.

One of Mona's greatest contributions during my tenure as Director was the way in which she represented the library in its dealings with the Research Library Group. Resource sharing is not an arrangement warmly embraced by many classical collection developers. Developing rather than sharing collections is what motivates the builders of great collections. But Mona was an exception, she knew that no matter how much we tried or how much we spent to acquire materials, we could never meet all the needs of our scholars. To her mind, RLG's resource sharing program represented an important supplement to our local collections. She worked diligently to show how our collections related to those of RLG colleague institutions. These relationships once identified often influenced her selection decisions. I believe her attitudes about shared collection development and resource sharing were very much ahead of her time.

It was a distinct pleasure to have had the opportunity to work with Mona East. She was tolerant of some of my "so-called management" notions, and I learned a great deal from her about the collections at the University and about how best to go about building a distinguished collection.

Richard M. Dougherty
Professor of Library Science
School of Information and
   Library Studies
University of Michigan,
   Ann Arbor

Introduction

Collection development as a sub-discipline of librarianship grew out of a need to systematize the selection and acquisition of library materials to more fully meet the needs of the library's users. In public and school libraries, librarians always have been the collection developers, but that was not the case in academic libraries, where traditionally faculty were the library collection developers. As faculty became professionalized and more demanding of library collections, they were also being replaced by librarians as the major selectors of library materials, thus plunging academic librarians more fully into collection development.

Collection development then referred primarily to analysis of, or at least knowledge of, existing collections, and selection and acquisition of new materials. Ancillary concerns related to the handling of non-print materials, censorship, and the vagaries of the publishing trade. Even the most recently published books on collection development tend to focus almost exclusively on these areas.

But in the last decade another, broader, term has begun to replace collection development in the language of library collections experts. That term is *collection management*.

The collection management concept grew from the recognition that neither library budgets nor facilities currently in place could absorb the proliferating materials available, and the suspicion that they should not try. Librarians who were used to mass selection/acquisition methods such as approval plans began talking in terms of co-operative management of collections among libraries. Even librarians in libraries that had never been able to afford such mass purchasing felt themselves squeezed in ways that were new and unexpected. Accelerating changes in storage and communications technology prompted librarians to look at their collections and ask how such technologies could fit with traditional materials and what their implementation would do to tra-

ditional library collections. In addition, they finally began to face the fact that library materials can be incredibly fragile and extraordinary efforts may be required to preserve even part of them for future generations. And that brought librarians right back to questions of budgets and storage.

As we move toward the end of the century, collection managers often find themselves in uncharted territory. Many are experimenting with new budgetary, administrative, analytical, technological, and co-operative configurations. As previously accepted norms and assumptions have proven inadequate to deal with new problems, managing the collections of even moderate-sized libraries has become a precarious endeavor.

If all of this makes the faint-hearted turn aside, it is exciting for those willing to take up the challenge of collection management, and collection management has become a major focus—some would say the chief focus—of attention in libraries.

Although no single volume could provide a comprehensive review of all collection management issues, as well as the responses and philosophies that surround them, it is intended here to suggest the range of those responses and philosophies in ways that will provoke readers to thought and/or action. We have brought together a group of librarians—not all of them collection managers by title, but all vitally interested in library collections and active in the collection management field—and asked them to talk about the issues that concern them most. As a result, a variety of issues are examined, each from the standpoint of someone who has been in a position to develop his or her own responses. These responses may not always be generic ones that would be transferable to all other libraries, and that is not their intention. Their purpose is to stimulate discussion and provide a starting point for decision-making.

The chapters are varied in scope and approach, a reflection of the various notions of collection management itself. Taken together, they provide a panorama of issues and responses. A knowledge of what collection managers are facing and how they are responding will perhaps bring collection management into clearer focus.

Symptomatic of the changing concept of collection management is the organizational framework within which collection management is now being handled in libraries. In "Organization of Collection Development and Management in Academic Libraries: a Pragmatic View," Carolyn Bucknall discusses some possible configurations to handle expanding collection management responsibilities and the changing and expanding knowledge base. Although her expertise, and thus her article, relates particularly to large academic libraries, the same type of problems and the same variety of responses can be seen in other kinds of libraries as well.

The expanding knowledge base is also the focus of Joseph Branin's "Information Policy for Collection Development Librarians," in which the author writes that as sources of information and its retrieval grow more and more complex, the need for definitions of information policy grows more and more acute. Developing strategies for the coordination of information sources, as well as dealing with a variety of cost structures and complex ownership and use arrangements, are prime subjects for such policies.

Budgeting issues loom large in all areas of collection management. In "Budgeting for Collection Development: a Suggestion," Richard Ring takes a second look at the structure and mechanisms of the budget allocation process and suggests how the allocation of the acquisitions budget can be linked to collection development, particularly book selection and collection evaluation, in specific and positive ways.

One of the most talked-about areas of collection management is cooperation between libraries. Though mechanisms for such cooperation have been in place for some time, Paul Mosher, in "Cooperative Collection Development: Collaborative Interdependence," points out that most libraries still strive for self-sufficient, or comprehensive, collections. He suggests that cooperative collection development will not become a reality until librarians really collaborate, not only on structural and mechanical levels, but on social and cultural ones as well.

Although collection managers have recognized for some time the need to evaluate their collections, evaluative techniques are by definition dependent on subjective elements. No sure-fire evaluative techniques are in place, although many libraries have developed methods that they feel serve them well. In "Collection Evaluation in the Research Environment," Ferne B. Hyman writes of the continuing work of developing meaningful and useful strategies for evaluation.

Margaret Byrnes, in "Preservation and Collection Management: Some Common Concerns," argues for linking preservation with collection management, not only theoretically, but in day-to-day decision-making. Touching on financing, planning, technological developments, and questions of access and copyright, she shows why collection management should be preservation-minded, and why preservation experts should be collection-oriented.

New technologies in libraries might be compared to the Trojan horse. Welcomed at first for the innovations that they allow, information technologies also are bringing challenges to library management, as well as to library budgets, and those challenges have forever changed the way users and librarians alike look at libraries. In "Information Technologies and Collection Management," Jutta Reed-Scott addresses some of the characteristics of that changing environment.

Any library, no matter its purpose or size, finds itself facing a crisis in serials management as serials proliferate and serials prices rise to breathtaking levels. As a result, collection managers have been looking for ways to keep serials budgets from taking over library materials budgets completely. Sara C. Heitshu and J. Travis Leach, in "Developing Serials Collections in the 1990s" pull this issue into the mainstream of collection management by speaking to the ways in which serials problems have, indeed, become collection problems.

Libraries, when all is said and done, are only as good as their users find them. Librarians often think of library users as people who come in occasionally, use library resources more or less successfully and then leave to carry out the main part of their business. But for some users, the library *is* the main part of their business. For researchers whose primary materials are in the library, the library is their laboratory. In "A Museum of the Book," Robert Super speaks for many such researchers as he compares the library to the chemist's laboratory or the paleontologists's museum. He reminds librarians that beyond all the technology and all the jargon are researchers who depend on librarians to maintain library/laboratories that researchers find useful, convenient, and responsive to their sometimes quite unpredictable needs.

In "Alexandria Revisited: Another Look at Questions of Space and Growth," Sheila Dowd does indeed take another look, and challenges what has become the conventional wisdom of many collection managers—cooperative collecting within the research library field.

If there is a theme running through these chapters, it is that collection managers should approach their responsibilities with care and caution because their work has an impact not only on their own collections, but on that part of the universe of knowledge that libraries are able to capture. Collection managers cannot afford to make uninformed assumptions about their collections, their relation to that larger universe, or the users who may, indeed, mistake the one for the other.

Organization of Collection Development and Management In Academic Libraries

by Carolyn Bucknall

Academic librarians are being bombarded with an accelerating stream of *news: new* services, *new* public relations, *new* information formats, *new* technologies and *new* catalogs have been introduced during the past 10 to 15 years. Innovations are not always successfully assimilated by large academic libraries and dislocations associated with change in one department often affect the entire library. Coping strategies have been envisioned and even implemented, but usually are grafted onto existing, traditional organizational structures. Therefore, collection development and management in academic libraries is most sensibly addressed in terms of the larger library organization.

THE LARGER FRAMEWORK

Organizational structures have not yet responded effectively to new directions opened as the knowledge base undergoes profound changes. We understand the notion that the printed word is not the only useful medium of intellectual exchange, although we don't always accept it. A limited legitimacy is accorded to sound recordings, nonprint visual materials (slides, photographs, microfilms, video and motion pictures), and now to numerical and textual databases in electronic format (online, ontape, disk or CD-ROM). Multimedia constructs yet undeveloped are the subjects of intense speculation. As potential for fast document delivery is realized, and as electronic networks truly become the academic *via franca*, the very character of libraries will be significantly altered. This assumes, of course, that academic libraries wish to embrace these new systems. Here is a monumental challenge for our profession.

We have been thoroughly warned to expect organizational consequences of change. We have been less successful in anticipating the precise nature of those consequences. New functions have been added, but very little formal restructuring has been undertaken to reflect new relationships that cut across organizational lines.

When the formal organization chart is not relevant to actual needs, alternate routes and interrelationships are developed by the staff. Actual needs and *new worker*[1] interests are officially acknowledged by creating standing committees, councils, and taskforces with librarywide membership, to gather and analyze information and make decisions. These bodies, while now a staple in academic library administration, are rarely shown on organization charts, perhaps because it is difficult to map their relationships as traditional hierarchies. Multiple reporting lines, a relatively new phenomenon,[2] are another—potentially more significant—departure from the norm.

A functionally interdependent and changeable library environment is the larger context in which this complex, dynamic system operates. Some of the components relevant to current academic library administration are selectively identified in the following paragraphs as: dislocation, communication, imitation, and automation.

Frequently what we have in academic libraries is a case of too much, too soon. Too much to absorb in the way of new ideas, too soon to adequately prepare staff for the change. Too much

> When the formal organization chart is not relevant to actual needs, alternate routes are developed by the staff

Carolyn Bucknall is Assistant Director for Collection Development at the General Libraries, University of Texas at Austin.

for staff to accomplish, given their existing duties. Too soon because traditional organizational structures cannot absorb so many simultaneous changes. Often, organizational dislocation results. Pressures are unevenly distributed. Developments in one area may be totally unknown or unfelt in another. A nascent *esprit* may transcend organizational lines when certain functions are shared, for example online searching or collection development. But sometimes the sharing becomes a source of discord. ("How come *they* don't serve at the Reference Desk too?") By and large the branch librarian is still ignorant of the difficulties and issues in contemporary cataloging, and the cataloger is still suspicious of the collection developer's right to assign cataloging priorities. Administrators can also be caught in the same knowledge gap, and for the same reasons. Indeed, administrators are perhaps the foremost among overworked librarians pressured by simultaneous changes and the need to respond to several clamorous constituencies at once. Organizational health is at risk, with the threat that stressed relationships will predominate.

Learning basic library functions was simpler when nothing ever changed. Now, education and communication is more difficult and more important than ever. Communication paths can be blazed through the organizational structure, whether informing one area about the functions of another, whether encouraging the director to reevaluate a particular library area, or whether educating the university administration on the importance of funding the online catalog. But effective communication also hinges on good leadership, management style, and imaginative use of a variety of communication devices.

With rapid change in society as well as in libraries, has come a degree of sophistication that no one could have foretold 30 years ago. Public relations is a case in point. Slick, intelligently written publications are effective public relations tools for furthering the library's objectives with the university administration, the library user, the potential donor, and even the library staff.

Another dynamic at work in library administration is the drive to imitate. We librarians may not know everything about our own libraries, but we are very sensitive to what is going on at others. When they *get ahead,* we are quick to follow. We must stay at the cutting edge. This is the "monkey see, monkey do" syndrome. Worthy programs apparently successful at other libraries are frequently imitated without adequate attention to staffing requirements or to dislocations produced in ongoing programs.

A rash of user-instruction programs introduced in the '70s raised people's expectations to an impossibly high level, given limited staff. But user instruction was nothing compared to the demands generated by the *new technology.* The point is not that user instruction is unworthy or that online databases are somehow wrong; the point is that staff (and budget, too) can support only so many add-ons. Somewhere along the line we become too stretched, edgy, resentful, prone to blame someone—perhaps colleagues whose workloads we have misunderstood—for our plight. Where is the leader who will bravely cut a program to relieve resources overload? Then the rest of us monkeys can follow with lightened burdens and refreshed spirits.

Mention should be made of two elements well-recognized as prime movers in any dynamic system of organization. First, is the *new worker,*[3] an employee whose values and expectations of the workplace are different from those of his predecessors. This worker likes to help determine the procedures and policies that shape his work and values a congenial work situation over higher salaries. Second is automation as an agent for organizational change. As automation impacts all areas of library activity, we gain insights into changes underway, even when their ultimate outcome is not perfectly clear. Most agree, however, that automated systems promote greater interdependence and reduce centralized processes and controls.[4] When the latter have grown beyond their capacity to operate efficiently, this process is accelerated.

Many other considerations could be mentioned. An extensive range of economic factors, for example, is not addressed here, political forces are dealt with only indirectly and limitations of physical facilities and logistics must be considered. Such factors, interacting in dynamic systems, are being explored increasingly in strategic planning and ultimately must be thoroughly analyzed in order to build effective organizational structures.

In summary, libraries are undergoing numerous changes, many simultaneously. Most profound, the character of the knowledge base itself is changing, and many of us foresee that the library will emerge from its metamorphosis with a form as yet unknown. Immense staffing pressures have been generated by increasing user expectations and add-on programs, while automation has produced, is producing, and will continue to produce more decentralized functions. At the same time, a greater interdependence is not accommodated by traditional organizational structures. Even when the organization chart appears the same, interrelationships in fact are much more complex. It is in this context that the organization of the collection development function must be considered.

CURRENT PATTERNS

Current concepts of collection development and management were introduced into academic libraries only during the last 20 to 25 years. We have come to identify the components of this function as selection, faculty liaison, collection management (including preservation), collection evaluation, fund management, and library use instruction—or collection interpretation.[5] Even as we have done so, we recognize that we are describing the past better than the future.

Collection development was not born in that simpler period when library functions could be learned only once. It is, from the perspective of many professionals, another add-on program. It does not often enjoy an entrenched constituency within the library, though support from faculty has been typically strong. However, the importance of collection development is increasingly being recognized. Thirteen years ago, only three ARL (Association for Research Libraries) member libraries showed a dedicated staff position for an assistant director or coordinator for collection development. In 1986 at least 34 of 61 organization charts in the ARL Office of Management Studies SPEC Kit no. 129 noted such a position.[6] The same survey showed 52 percent of collection development officers report to the director, and Jeanne Sohn recently cited 74 percent.[7]

The type of organization likely to have a collection development function is determined by several factors, most of which relate to size: size of the collection, size of the book budget, and size of professional and support staff. Generally, the smaller the library, the smaller the collection development program. In evolutionary phases, responsibility may migrate from the director to the head of acquisitions or reference, to a collection development coordinator or head of a collection development department, and finally to an assistant or associate director. Bonita Bryant[8] describes the process very well. Only when a library has evolved to naming one person responsible for overseeing the collection development and management function can it be placed on an organization chart.

No consensus is apparent on where, organizationally, the collection management and development program belongs. It can be solely a staff function reporting to the director. It can be a line function, or a coordinated function attached to technical services, public services, or a department within these areas, it can be dismembered and scattered among the various departments. Conversely, according to Sohn,[9] other functions can be subsumed by the collection development and management programs, the most common being acquisitions and preservation.

A centralized *vs.* a coordinated model for collection development organization has been debated for the past two decades. Centralized collection development in its purest form, staffed by bibliographers[10] whose sole responsibility is collection development, and whose reporting line leads to only one box on the organization chart, exists in few academic libraries. It confers certain obvious advantages:

- individual bibliographer workloads can be monitored to assure adequate time for successful performance
- individual bibliographer performance can be evaluated more easily
- projects can be undertaken more easily because of greater staff flexibility
- strong *esprit* develops within the unit, and there is greater opportunity for prestige as a group
- individual bibliographers are subject only to their own limitations: professional abilities, knowledge of subject specialty, organizational skills, and personal attributes (e.g. initiative, interpersonal skills, etc.)
- excellent opportunity for intellectual accomplishment and job satisfaction.

Offsetting these advantages is one serious difficulty: a troublesome tendency to insulate bibliographers from the *new technology* and from the rest of the staff.[11] This can be exacerbated by competitive hierarchical structures that discourage exploration of shared interests and efforts toward functional integration. When any librarian loses touch with recent and ongoing advances in the field, the entire organization suffers a loss. When a whole group loses touch, its effectiveness is considerably diminished and unless the underlying causes are dealt with, further decline may occur.

A coordinated collection development and management organization, in which bibliographers spend only a portion of their time on this function and the remainder on primary responsibilities in another department, has its drawbacks:

- without line responsibility the coordinator may lack authority necessary to manage the program
- the coordinator may not have control over the time bibliographers spend on collection development and management
- the coordinator may not have a role in bibliographer performance evaluation
- the coordinator's position may be perceived as less prestigious than one who sits on top of a pyramid
- the coordinated program will not have built-in communication linkages

We librarians may not know everything about our own libraries, but we are very sensitive to what is going on at others

- a coordinated program lacks the flexibility of staff dedicated, full time, to collection development
- individual bibliographers may be frustrated due to conflicting demands on worktime by primary and collection development responsibilities.

Most of these disadvantages can be mitigated by various strategems. For example, having the coordinator report to the director can boost prestige, as can positioning the job at a relatively high level on the organization chart. Of course, the power of the purse is a wonderful authority enhancer; when the coordinator controls fund allocation, many obstacles dwindle.

Some advantages of a coordinated model are:

- part time bibliographers, especially in smaller libraries, may be the only staff available to make a collection development and management program possible
- bibliographers with primary responsibilities are more likely to be aware of the latest advances in their field
- bibliographer responsibilities enhance job satisfaction and the possibility for intellectual accomplishment in subject areas.

Lack of a single, predominant organizational model for collection management and development has been noted in library literature. Sohn has sketched a composite of a typical ARL collection development and management unit. It is composed of a group of bibliographers with multiple subject assignments who report to the collection development officer or to someone else with dedicated collection development responsibilities. This group is complemented by other bibliographers with more limited subject responsibilities, whose primary assignment is in another functional area of the library.[12] Individuals in the second group may have dual reporting lines: to their department heads in their primary capacity and to the collection development head in their capacity as bibliographers. Presumably the collection development officer would have more control over such critical matters as time spent on collection management and development and performance evaluation. A composite model might require coordination, rather than actual line responsibility, on the part of the collection development officer. Apart from this distinction the composite model shares in the best and worst features of the centralized and the coordinated models.

Whether the object is to restructure the collection development and management function or to improve its management within an existing structure, several helpful administrative tools are noteworthy. Compiling a bibliographer's manual can clarify expectations and is extremely beneficial for both process and product.[13] A formal training program using the manual as a primary tool and including an extended mentor-protege relationship, is an effective introduction to the program.[14] Groups of bibliographers working in their disciplines with similar characteristics, each headed by a coordinator, can achieve a more integrated approach to collection development and management in a large, dispersed organization. When a central core of full-time bibliographers is maintained, their duties often relate to publications from (and sometimes about) a particular geographical area. Typically such a group is expanded by bibliographers who are also catalogers, a natural union of language and area expertise.

Whatever organization form is chosen, a clear understanding of administrative relationships is essential. The best qualified bibliographers must be recruited—whether people already on the staff or from outside the library. They must have enough time to do what bibliographers are supposed to do, as well as adequate support staff, and a good training program. An excellent system of communication that is reciprocal in every possible direction is one of the tools that will help accomplish these things.

More than one organizational pattern can be effective. The ultimate test of any organization is whether it works. In order to pass this test the structure must first be appropriate to its context, with due consideration of the organization's health, traditions and prestige, as well as the management style of the director and other members of the library administration. Internal political factors will also determine where and how collection development and management fits into the structure; for example, the nature of competing programs, their public visibility, the immediacy of the needs they serve, etc. Add to these the director's own agenda and perceptions, tempered perhaps by special interest groups such as library administrators, other staff members, vocal faculty, and certain influential members of the university administration.

Making an organizational structure work is essentially a political process involving education, statesmanship, diplomacy, and an arsenal of other positive attributes. We all have a role in that process.

FUTURE DIRECTIONS

Jeanne Sohn reports that, despite improvements in status, almost one-third of the collection development officers responding to her survey were dissatisfied with the way their libraries have organized collection development; those who expressed satisfaction but also made negative comments brought the total to almost 50 percent. And this although 81 percent of Sohn's 93 respondents indicated that a change in structure or organizational placement of the collection development unit had already occurred in the past ten years.[15]

Possibly collection developers' dissatisfaction with current organizational structures has less to do with collection development than with the total library context.

Take a hypothetical model of a composite collection development organization: an amalgam of full-time bibliographers in a collection development department and part-time bibliographers in a reference department. Overload has spurred reference librarians and allies to campaign for drawing full-time bibliographer colleagues into reference service, not for *online information* retrieval but for *reference desk* duty. Full-time bibliographers, of course, respond with indignant resistance. Polarities between the two groups are expressed as elitism and populism, and the argument proceeds as follows:

Full-time Bibliographers: Given that reference has more work than it can do—much of it self-imposed—why should full-time bibliographers be made to share in the misery by serving time at the general reference desk where predominantly undergraduate students ask repetitive and nonchallenging questions? It may be populist to reduce the intellectual level at which all staff must serve to the lowest common denominator, but is it sensible? Why not undertake to raise the general intellectual environment of all librarians?

Part-time Bibliographers/Reference Librarians: Reference desk service will give full-time bibliographers meaningful (and currently lacking) contact with library users, on which collection development decisions can be based. This will be tremendously helpful to the bibliographer and will at the same time permit broader contribution of his/her subject expertise. Also, it seems unfair that full-time bibliographers have more time to evaluate collections, establish meaningful communication with faculty, and undertake extensive projects related to preservation. *Why should full-time bibliographers be free to come and go as they choose?*

The dynamics of the larger organizational context are at work, with a complex array of opposing pressures and interests. Do we take this marriage proposal seriously? Is a wedding inevitable? Does service at the reference desk really enhance bibliographers' performance? Is a new elite (those possessing the keys to online information) in the making?

Considering the situation in current organizational terms, the following points might be raised.

The proposal, which is symptomatic of some degree of dislocation, must be given serious attention, with diagnosis pending further examination. Routine reference desk service as an aid to collection development and management seems an unsubstantiated claim developed to reduce reference workloads. As such, it may be a further indicator of stress, or, when advocated by nonbibliographer staff, ignorance of the collection development and management function. It would seem more appropriate to examine reference workloads, programs, and constituencies to identify changes needed for reference, not collection development.

Other rationales for joining the collection development function with the reference department might be more compelling. If such a union were to occur, collection development would undoubtedly lose some of its clout, some of its activities would be curtailed, and some of its goals ignored. On the other hand, full-time bibliographers might benefit by swimming into the library mainstream and connecting with current technological advances. The collection development and management program (along with reference) might derive at least limited benefits from such a recasting of the library organization.

Reasoning of this sort helps us to understand underlying organizational forces and sometimes improves operations, but essentially it perpetuates traditional organizational concepts. Thus, while six ARL libraries have recently moved from the centralized to the composite organizational model, five have moved in the opposite direction.[16] The dissatisfactions noted by Sohn are likely to continue until we rethink the basis for our organizational structures.

The case of overworked reference librarians who want to tap collection development staff could have led to an entirely different approach to organization. Had a more integrated role for all librarians been sought, with individual performance at the highest level possible, reorganization of public services, collection development, *and* other functions would have been considered. Charles Osburn has theorized that collection development and management is central to library operations and pivotal in library-community relations.[17] This strong voice on its behalf coming from the Research Libraries Group has done much to underscore its value to library services in general and to cooperative ventures in preservation and resource sharing in particular. If collection development is indeed central, it is in a good position to help restructure traditional library functions into more effective organizational patterns.

Osburn, noting the decreasing importance of

No consensus is apparent on where, organizationally, the collection management and development program belongs

Making an organizational structure work is essentially a political process involving education, statesmanship, diplomacy, and an arsenal of other positive attributes

resources ownership in most libraries, suggests that future directions will be characterized by looking outward to community needs, rather than inward to the collection as traditionally conceived. The role of information and service broker remains to be assumed by collection development librarians, for if not, "it will be by other professions, and librarians will continue to be responsible only for maintenance of an intellectual utility, subordinate to the other group."[18] He further asserts that "the shift of emphasis from collection-oriented goals, eventually to process-oriented goals . . . will permit collection development to function most successfully in the future."[19]

As we begin to make this transition, we can be informed by two existing models, each representing an evolutionary step toward a new kind of structure. Branch libraries in large academic systems have typically been quick to explore new relationships with clientele as the knowledge base has evolved. Insights into the *new collection development* are emerging in these academic library settings. A more mature model, the medical library, delivers highly sophisticated and constantly changing information services. Among characteristics shared by the two models are: a focused environment with well defined subject scope, a readily identified library user community, library subject specialists who offer integrated information services with a high degree of involvement in the research process, and relatively small organizational units that exemplify integrated rather than centralized functions. The advantages of small teams as a basic unit of organization have been noted in industry as particularly suited to both the demands of the new worker and functional integration resulting from automation.[20]

A function as reconceptualized might, for example, be the provision of integrated information services for those engaged in advanced research. In the press of public services activity begun in the '60s and continuing into the future, services to researchers in particular have been sometimes neglected and frequently fragmented. Today—at least in the central or research library—most bibliographers select and manage print and audio-visual research materials, and reference librarians select and administer electronic databases useful in research, while individual researchers are often assisted in an uncoordinated fashion, primarily in response to specific queries. Looking at new scholarly systems we are struck by the need to maintain a core of subject specialists who are also experts on available library resources in all formats, cognizant of research trends and methods, conversant with hardware, software, and scholarly networks, and interested in being more involved in the research process. Bibliographers and other specialists could join together in libraries organized to give in-depth support services for advanced research.

Organizational experimentation is one of the lesser-used tools available to us. While librarians are generally not regarded as risk-takers, several organizational innovations have now come to represent the norm. Using such tools as multiple reporting lines, councils, clusters, teams, tribes, etc., we can create different organizational structures that more realistically reflect existing and emerging relationships; structures that facilitate rather than impede communication. Significant organizational regrouping has been rare among large academic libraries, with the notable exception of the University of Illinois.[21] We need to know more about the lessons of such ventures. Still, the organizational response to tomorrow's environment may be largely independent of the past.

Ironically, libraries may run the greatest risk by avoiding risk. Hazards are real, but potential gains are great.

References

1. Robert W. Goddard, "Motivating the Modern Employee," *Management World* 12 (Sept. 1983), p. 8.
2. *Organization Charts in ARL Libraries,* SPEC Kit, no. 129. (Washington: Systems and Procedures Exchange Center, Association of Research Libraries, Office of Management Studies, Nov.–Dec. 1986).
3. Goddard, "Motivating," p. 8.
4. Richard E. Walton and Gerald I. Susman, "People Policies for the New Machines," *Harvard Business Review* 87 (March–Apr. 1987), p. 98–99.
5. University of Texas at Austin, General Libraries, *Bibliographer's Manual: a Guide to the General Libraries Collection Development Program* (Austin: 1982), p. 7.
6. *Organization Charts in ARL Libraries,* SPEC Kit no. 129.
7. Jeanne Sohn, "Collection Development Organizational Patterns in ARL Libraries," *Library Resources and Technical Services* 31 (April/June 1987), p. 125.
8. Bonita Bryant, "The Organizational Structure of Collection Development," *Library Resources and Technical Services* 31 (April/June 1987), p. 113–114.
9. Sohn, "Organizational Patterns," p. 131
10. The term *bibliographer* is applied throughout this paper to "a library staff member, typically possessing superior knowledge of a discipline, whose responsibilities include aspects of development and management of the library's information resources in the subject field(s) of his or her specialization; also referred to as a selector, subject specialist, or collection developer." This definition is

taken from *Guide for Writing a Bibliographer's Manual* (Chicago: Resources and Technical Services Division, American Library Association) [in press].

11. This trend toward "maintaining a professional preserve evolved into a mechanism of defense against questioning from outside the designated collection development area . . . In some libraries . . . the trajectory of this professionally inspired movement led dangerously close to stasis in a function that should be the most dynamic of enterprises," according to Charles B. Osburn, "Toward a Reconceptualization of Collection Development," in *Advances in Library Administration and Organization* (Greenwood, Conn: JAI Press. 1983), v. 2, p. 180.

12. Sohn, "Organizational Patterns," p. 131.

13. University of Texas at Austin, General Libraries, *Bibliographer's Manual*, p. 2.

14. Scott R. Bullard, "Educating Rita—Part II: Training For Collection Development," *Library Acquisitions: Practice and Theory* 8 (1984), p. 244–245.

15. Sohn, "Organizational Patterns," p. 130.

16. *Collection Development Organization and Staffing,* SPEC Kit no. 131. (Washington: Systems and Procedures Exchange Center, Association of Research Libraries, Office of Management Studies, Feb. 1987).

17. Charles B. Osburn, "Toward a Reconceptualization of Collection Development," in *Advances in Library Administration and Organization* (Greenwood, Conn: JAI Press, 1983), v. 2, p. 183.

18. Osburn, "Reconceptualization," p. 183.

19. *Ibid.*

20. Walton and Susman. "People Policies," *Harvard Business Review* 87 (March–Apr. 1987), p. 99–100.

21. The University of Illinois Libraries has recently regrouped on the basis of subject rather than function. As related to a particular subject, the total range of current library activities—collection development and management, acquisition, cataloging and interpretive services—are performed by a single individual.

Information Policies for Collection Development Librarians

by Joseph J. Branin

Beware of "Info-Smoke" warns Art Plotnick in a recent *American Libraries* editorial. It clouds the meaning and purpose of libraries by embroiling them in the "world's hottest commodity"— information.[1] "The information age" or "the information society" are clichés used with abandon by many librarians. "Information" is the buzzword for grant applications, articles, and new names for libraries and library schools. As Plotnick rhetorically asks, "Who *isn't* in the information business?"

Underlying the current preoccupation with information, whether couched in terms of "information handling," "information storage and retrieval," "information centers," or "information policy," is a legitimate need for a better definition and broader understanding of how the content of knowledge is organized, preserved, and communicated. In libraries this means expanding responsibility beyond the traditional information boundaries of published print or print-derived materials into new formats of electronic data, images, and sounds. Therefore it means a change in the way libraries deliver information to users. Collections of material that are housed on-site and owned by libraries are being supplemented by information sources that are remote but rapidly accessed using new delivery systems.

Collection development librarians are vitally involved in many aspects of the information business. They are responsible for building and managing the library's resource base, and their activities should be guided by a written collection development policy. This document also serves as an information policy for the library, describing collection strengths and weaknesses, and formats and subjects emphasized or avoided. However, an examination of most libraries' collection development policies would show that bibliographers are asked to focus almost exclusively on collections of owned print and print-derived resources. Such materials now make up the bulk of library collections, certainly in research libraries, and will for years to come. But in this new information age, collection development librarians must look beyond their traditional shelving to a world of computer screens and databases. They must link their collection development policies with campus-wide and national information policy.

Barbara Moran in *Academic Libraries: The Changing Knowledge Centers of Colleges and Universities* predicts a shift away from collections toward information access. According to Moran, "As time goes on, print sources will constitute a diminished proportion of the total information available for scholarly purposes, and as this trend progresses, librarians will deal more with 'information' than with books."[2]

To date, however, the introduction of computer technology has not diminished the output of print resources. As Irving Horowitz points out in *Communicating Ideas: The Crisis of Publishing in a Post-Industrial Society*, "There is nothing in the evidence to suggest that the flow of print has contracted under the impact of the new technology."[3] Book production figures and book publishing revenues continue to rise. For example, book publishing revenues have steadily grown from less than $500 million in 1950, to more than $2.9 billion in 1970, and over $7.0 billion in 1980.[4]

> ... collection development librarians must help create a system that organizes and links all information sources, whether traditional or new, print or electronic

Joseph J. Branin is Director of Humanities/Social Sciences Libraries at the University of Minnesota.

Electronic information is not replacing print formats, it is sustaining and expanding the information explosion of post-industrial society. Not only is there more print information available, but other formats are emerging as effective and popular carriers of information as well. Collection development librarians have been trying for some time to contend with the print information explosion. Even the largest research libraries cannot hope to be self-sufficient. No single library can provide all the research material its clientele may need. To overcome this limitation, libraries have banded together on a local, regional, or national level to form cooperative networks for resource sharing and document delivery. Membership in the Research Libraries Group, OCLC, the Center for Research Libraries, or any number of regional or local consortia is an important element in a library's information capacity.

However, the challenge of managing information services today extends beyond cooperative collection development and interlibrary loan programs. As Patricia Battin states in "The Library: Center of the Restructured University," librarians now face a dual challenge: "we must provide new structures of access to knowledge in an increasing variety of formats and, at the same time, continue to preserve, manage, and make available scholarly information in the traditional printed formats with appropriate links between all formats."[5] Collection development librarians cannot abandon their commitment to the book, the journal, and the microform, but they must extend their range to include computer software and access to local and remote databases. Most important, collection development librarians must help create a system or infrastructure that organizes and links all information sources, whether traditional or new, print or electronic.

AN INFORMATION POLICY

An information policy is essential to define information sources and means of access to them throughout an organization or community, just as a collection development policy is meant to guide the selection and management of library material. Advances in technology have created a decentralized and fragmented information environment. In addition to libraries, computer centers, commercial database vendors, and individual researchers now have the ability to compile and retrieve vast stores of information.

What role can or should collection development librarians play in this new information-rich environment? One important part is to identify and organize various formats and sources of infor-

mation important to a specific discipline. For example, at the University of Georgia, the library's Social Sciences Bibliographer, James Kuhlman, found that databases needed by his faculty were available on campus but often inaccessible. Writing in *American Libraries*, Kuhlman describes a situation commonly found on campuses: "Research libraries have left it up to computer centers to deal with the machine-readable materials. Computer centers in turn left it to users to find, purchase, and maintain their own materials. Data sets were viewed as the personal possessions of individuals; cataloging of data sets was ignored. Faculty in the same department and different state agencies often bought the same, expensive tapes, only to lose and forget about them."[6]

CENTRALIZED SERVICES

Kuhlman, working with social science faculty and computer center staff, changed this fragmented situation by centralizing services in the library. Control of local membership in the Interuniversity Consortium for Political and Social Research, which collects and makes available a variety of numeric databases, was moved from the Political Science Department to the library. The University's Computer Center transferred staff and responsibility for the servicing of census data tapes to the library, and plans were made to move the Business School's database operations to the library. In this example, the library took responsibility for the acquisition and cataloging of social sciences databases and for patron assistance in using them, while the Computer Center handled storage and technical servicing of the tapes.

On a larger scale, Columbia University is planning to integrate all information services on its campus. According to Columbia's former Vice President and University Librarian, Patricia Battin, "The very diversity of scholarly inquiry and information needs requires in the electronic age an unprecedented degree of centralized, coordinated linkages and compatibilities to serve that diversity and permit the autonomy necessary for productive and creative scholarship."[7] Information services at Columbia will be centralized in a "Scholarly Information Center" which will merge the library and the Computer Center. Such centralization and integration will, according to Battin, "provide one-stop shopping for the University community as well as a stabilizing planning mechanism for effective and flexible response to rapidly changing technologies."[8]

Formulating an information policy need not imply any particular organization of information services. Centralized services is just one of many options available. Richard Dougherty, Director of Libraries at the University of Michigan, cautions librarians about their fascination with merging libraries and computer centers. According to Dougherty, the organization of libraries and computer centers differs greatly and "models that rely on coordination and collaboration are more likely to predominate in the near term than models that subordinate one unit to another."[9] Instead of merging the two units, Dougherty recommends careful cooperation between the library and computer center through the use of joint working groups.[10]

Developing a strategy for coordinating or integrating diverse information sources, whether in a single institution or among a group of libraries, is an important policy issue, but not the only one that collection development librarians will have to address. If information has become "the world's hottest commodity," one can be certain that questions of costs, ownership, and access will also be at the forefront of consideration.

INFORMATION: WHO PAYS?

Information has never really been free, but new technology makes the question of who pays more difficult to answer. Should information sources and services be funded centrally and then distributed to users free of charge? Or should users be assessed per-item fees for their access to information, an option that is readily available with computerized information retrieval?[11] Ideally the traditional library model should prevail, where a communal policy allows free access to collections and reference services. In reality, however, more and more costs associated with access to information are being passed on directly to users. Most libraries are charging for computerized search services, either to recover costs or to control demand, and most computer centers have always found it necessary to charge users for their services.

According to Donald Dunn, "One of the driving forces for change in information technology has been the evolutionary, steady reduction in cost in the computer and communication industries."[12] The availability of pocket calculators and inexpensive home computers is evidence of this trend. But the costs of introducing new information technology systems can still be quite high. As Richard Dougherty points out, "It is not unusual to hear of price tags approaching $50 million (or more for large campuses) when planning a fully computerized campus linked together by a telecommunications network."[13] Also, equipment must be maintained and upgraded, and software developed or purchased. For collection development librarians, who already are strapped for book and

journal funds, the prospect of adding new formats and in some cases paying for access to rather than ownership of information may not be encouraging.

There are no easy solutions to this situation. Collection development librarians must become involved in planning the economics of information services at their institutions. Computer software and electronic access to databases are not replacing the need for published print material. One should not be sacrificed for the other. Also, direct charges to users for certain types of information services should be examined carefully. What are the criteria for determining when a user should pay and when have free access to information? A policy that addresses these difficult economic issues will help avoid discrimination against a particular user group or against a certain information format.

INFORMATION: WHO OWNS IT?

Another important issue is that of ownership; information is a valuable market commodity. This issue is complex and can involve questions of censorship and intellectual freedom as well as property rights and privacy. It is both a national and local policy issue. Is information a "public good," that is, "a good that one user can consume without diminishing its availability or usefulness to another user"?[14] Or is it an "economic good," a commodity whose value will be lessened by free, unrestricted access? According to Donald Dunn, "Patents and copyrights create property rights in information and ideas with the objective of making investments in the creation of intellectual property more attractive, relative to investment in goods not subject to copying. Patents and copyrights not only protect the creator of new information from 'piracy' by others seeking to make copies, but also create transferable pieces of property that can be sold in the market, thus enhancing the value of new information by making it more like other goods."[15]

Collection development librarians are accustomed to purchasing books, journals, and microforms that then become the property of their libraries. These materials can be used freely and repeatedly by patrons, usually at no charge. Only copying significant portions of their content, not use, is restricted or controlled by copyright law. Some of the new information formats, however, do have more restrictions or controls over their use. Often the purchaser of a computer software package must agree to limit its use to a particular individual or location. Access to an online, full text database usually involves a fee for each use, and this practice may spread to traditional formats. Looking to

. . . librarians must play a vital role in forming a new structure that assures fair and open access to a great variety of information sources

Western Europe and to the control database vendors exercise over their products, authors and publishers of print material in the United States are lobbying for Public Lending Right legislation. If enacted, such legislation would mean an end to the tradition of free access to information in American libraries. The user or the library would be required to pay a fee each time an item is borrowed.[16]

The U.S. Federal government, the largest producer of information in the world, is also turning to a marketplace concept to control and reduce its data output. As part of its agenda to shrink the Federal government, the Reagan Administration tried to assign what were once public responsibilities to the private sector, a phenomenon labeled "privatization." The Office of Management and Budget's Circular A-130, issued in December 1985 after much criticism by librarians, directs government agencies to rely whenever possible on the private sector for the dissemination of government information and to follow an "only-disseminate-it-if-you-must" policy.[17] Examples of information programs of government agencies turned over to private contractors can be found in the Department of Agriculture, the Patent and Trademark Office, and the Environmental Protection Agency.[18] Librarians fear that such practice will restrict access to public, government information, because ownership is being transferred to the private sector where economic and property right controls will be exerted.

On the local level, questions of information ownership may result more from organizational turf or individual privacy issues then from political or economic considerations. Will university departments or individual researchers give up control of a database which they may have purchased with grant funds or compiled themselves? Is the database so idiosyncratic or personal that it does not belong in the public domain? Universities that have begun to prepare directories or catalogs of their campus databases face such questions. Collection development librarians must help their institutions construct policies regarding what are and are not appropriate public information sources.

Restricted access to information because of organizational inefficiencies, pricing, licensing agreements, privatization or parochialism goes against the grain of librarians' basic professional ethic of protecting intellectual freedom. The Council on Library Resources in 1985 issued a statement on Scholarship, Research, and Access to Information with the following introduction:

Those who are concerned with libraries and books have long recognized and often strongly asserted the

need for unconstrained access to information as a condition essential to every democratic society. The computer, telecommunications, and text storage technologies that now play a prominent and at times dominant role in many aspects of library service and information systems have created a very different and complicated new environment. The established structure is changing and powerful economic forces are having a profound influence on all aspects of scholarly communication, libraries, and information services generally. While technology is powerful and brings a promise of unmatched opportunities, it is essential to remember that ready access to information is not automatically assured. That goal must be constantly and aggressively pursued.[19]

SELECTION VS. CENSORSHIP

Collection development librarians know there is a fine line between selection and censorship. In fact, too much concentration on the selection activity of a collection development program can lead to censorship. Eric Moon made this point in *Book Selection and Censorship in the Sixties*. According to Moon "the principal reason why shelf collections are so frequently inadequate in meeting readers needs is that the book selection process stops too early, operates too much in limbo. Rare is the library where trained personnel are assigned fulltime to the care and study of the book collection and its usage."[20] To avoid one's own prejudices in the selection process, the collection development librarian must put that process in the context of a complete, well-organized collection management program. Collection development librarians must know their collections, must know their users, and they must follow a carefully prepared collection policy, if they are to select the best and most useful material for their libraries.

Much has changed in the 25 years since Moon wrote about selection and censorship. As the Council on Library Resources statement points out, the new information technology has "created a very different and complicated new environment." Just as collection development librarians must put their selection activities within the context of a broader management program, so too must they relate their library's traditional collections to the larger information environment. The established structure is changing, and collection development librarians must play a vital role in forming a new structure that assures fair and open access to a great variety of information sources. They can do this by actively participating in formulation of information policy on both the local and national levels, and keeping their eyes clear of "info smoke."

References

1. Art Plotnick, "Info-Smoke Gets in Your Eyes," *American Libraries,* 17 (Oct. 1986): 656.
2. Barbara Moran, *Academic Libraries: The Changing Knowledge Centers of Colleges and Universities* (Washington, D.C.: Association for the Study of Higher Education, 1984), 75.
3. Irving Louis Horowitz, *Communicating Ideas: The Crisis of Publishing in a Post-Industrial Society* (New York: Oxford University Press, 1986), 15.
4. Dan Lacey, "Publishing and the New Technology," *Books, Libraries and Electronics: Essays on the Future of Written Communications* (White Plains, N.Y.: Knowledge Industry Publications, 1982), 85.
5. Patricia Battin, "The Library: Center of the Restructured University," *College and Research Libraries,* 45 (May 1984): 172.
6. James R. Kuhlman and Everett S. Lee, "Data-Power to the People," *American Libraries,* 17 (Nov. 1986): 758.
7. Patricia Battin, "The Electronic Library - A Vision for the Future," *EDUCOM Bulletin,* 19 (Summer 1984): 13.
8. Ibid., 16–17.
9. Richard M. Dougherty, "Libraries and Computing Centers: A Blueprint for Collaboration," *College and Research Libraries,* 48 (July 1987): 290.
10. Ibid., 295.
11. Rowland Lorimer, "Implications of the New Technologies of Information," *Scholarly Publishing,* 16 (April 1985): 200.
12. Donald A. Dunn, "Information resources and the New Information Technologies: Implications for Public Policy," *Information Reports and Bibliographies,* 13 (1984): 7.
13. Dougherty, "Libraries and Computer Centers," 293.
14. Dunn, "Information Resources and the New Information Technologies," 8.
15. Ibid.
16. Horowitz, *Communicating ideas,* 80.
17. Task Force on Government Information in Electronic Formats, "Report No. 2" (Association of Research Libraries, Washington, D.C. 21 April 1987), 30.
18. Jeffrey L. Fox, "EPA Dumps Chemical Data System," *Science,* 226 (Nov. 16, 1984) 816.
19. Board of Directors, Council on Library Resources, "Scholarship, Research, and Access to Information: A Statement from the Council on Library Resources" (Council on Library Resources, Inc., Washington, D.C., January 1985).
20. Eric Moon, ed., *Book Selection and Censorship in the Sixties* (New York: R.R. Bowker Company, 1969), 11.

Budgeting for Collection Development: A Suggestion

by Richard Ring

Towards the middle of *The Name of the Rose* Adso of Melk realizes that "not infrequently books speak of books. . . . In the light of this reflection, the library seemed all the more disturbing to me. It was then the place of a long, centuries-old murmuring, an imperceptible dialogue between one parchment and another, a living thing, a receptacle of powers not to be ruled by a human mind, a treasure of secrets emanated by many minds, surviving the death of those who had produced them or had been their conveyors." With these thoughts in mind Adso asks his mentor William of Baskerville "what is the use of hiding books, if from the books not hidden you can arrive at the concealed ones?" William replies that "over the centuries it is no use at all. In a space of years or days it has some use. . . ." To which Adso, dumbfounded, asks "and is a library, then, an instrument not for distributing truth but for delaying its appearance?"[1]

A twentieth century librarian might disagree with this passage at first glance. Those engaged in collection development may chafe, or laugh, at the very notion that their efforts hide, or even hinder the dissemination of the truth. More prolonged reflection, however, suggests that William of Baskerville and even Adso, to his own surprise and ours, sensed the principles of collection development in the best of libraries.

In part, the role of collection development is to store away—conceal, if you will—books whose content some future researcher will reveal and use to uncover still other little-known books. In this process librarians both speed and delay the appearance of truth. This should disturb only those who believe that truth in the library exists and can be revealed *in toto*. Jorge Luis Borges ironically expresses this sentiment in the "Library of Babel": "on some shelf . . . there must exist a book which is the formula and perfect compendium of all the rest: some librarian has gone through it and he is analogous to a god."[2]

Collection development librarians are no gods and can operate only on the assumption that books are added to the library one at a time and that each added volume may help someone. In some libraries and for some subject areas books added have an immediate and predictable use. In many research libraries and for most of the humanities and social sciences books must be added to the collection whose use is neither immediate nor predictable. This process of storing away the undigested past for the benefit of an unknown future is perhaps the most crucial and least understood part of collection development.

WHAT'S IN A NAME?

In recent years the label "collection development" has been adopted widely by libraries of all types for activities that have long been conducted unnamed. Despite the fact that the principal indexing service for library-related material still eschews the term, the literature has many books and articles dealing with collection development. Much of this deals with matters of policy and the principles of book selection, although other formats are increasingly included. At its very heart collection development is, and always has been, a matter of selecting all sources of information most needed for a particular library.

Always implied, but not so frequently discussed, is the qualifying phrase: selecting those books most needed *within the budgetary resources of the library*. It is so obvious that one can acquire only

> A library's budget and how it is allocated may be the most significant single factor determining which and how many books a library acquires

Richard Ring is Collection Development Librarian at the University of Kansas.

the books one can pay for (or persuade someone to donate) that it has seemed hardly worth serious discussion. Only questions about formulae for allocations among various areas, subjects and departments has evoked a body of literature.[3] The structure and mechanisms of the budget are rarely discussed as key collection development issues. But they are just as important to the shape and quality of a library's collections as collection development policies and the selection of particular items. Moreover, the existing literature most often deals with dividing up the base budget and not with variable and one-time only funding.

This relative neglect reflects the fact that many librarians engaged in collection development, including some chief collection development officers, have less to say about the allocation of the materials budget than about selection policies. A library's budget and how it is allocated may be the most significant single factor determining which and how many books a library acquires. Faculty members understand this and often express their concern.

The decision to spend all, or most of the acquisitions budget on current imprints is an important collection development decision. The use of approval plans, blanket orders and other mass-gathering schemes further links budget with book selection. In our society, addicted as it is to the new and the news, acquiring large numbers of current imprints may be desirable and necessary. But librarians should recognize that this leaves most of the real decisions about the shape and character of their collections to publishers, booksellers and other agents.

TARGET AREAS

What I am proposing is that the structure of the budget allocation process take into consideration the needs of particular local collecting strengths. This is not a radical suggestion, such structures already exist in many libraries. On the basis of experience in the University of Kansas Libraries, however, I would like to carry the process a step further and propose a structure for the allocation of funds to specifically targeted collecting areas for limited periods of time. I believe that this is what Fred Lynden had in mind when he spoke of an allocated contingency fund "to relieve concern about historical aberrations in funding, and to satisfy major unanticipated needs."[4] Murray S. Martin advocates "the provision of enrichment funds for special collection development projects" to maintain budget flexibility and to be able to respond to change as well as particular needs.[5]

The University of Kansas Libraries have allocated funds on a one-time basis for special projects for several years. All have strengthened particular areas of the collection, helped bibliographers and provided general fiscal and collection development flexibility. For example, existing strong collections on Haiti and international feminism have been strengthened further by special project funding. Special allocations have been made for collections of literary manuscripts, right wing periodicals from the 1930s and 1940s, and nineteenth century Portuguese drama. Kansas and regional collections on black history and native American history have been enhanced. Finally, large amounts of material have been acquired for relatively new collections on the Vietnam experience, on sports in American history, on Japanese ceramics, and on German-Jewish culture in the twentieth century.

Organizing the materials budget to fund special projects for a limited period of time may benefit a library's collections in a number of different ways. Concentrated spending on a specific area can strengthen an existing collection or help to build a needed one. Almost every library has strengths in some local and regional subjects. Often these local collections have national significance because of their subject, size or unique holdings. If maintaining these collections is an on-going, long-term process, funding should be a regular part of the library's acquisitions budget. But often such collections need one-time money to fill in specifically identified gaps in the holdings or to take advantage of purchasing opportunities. If a limited amount of material is available in a given field, a one-time allocation can help to acquire a good portion of that material. Targeting specific areas in this way may benefit not only the local library's collection but also the amorphous, yet very real, national collection. When special project funds are used to purchase retrospectively from out-of-print catalogs, bibliographers usually will find that paying attention to the national collection will benefit the local library's collection as well. Acquiring older materials that few if any other libraries own or have cataloged frequently strengthens a specific collection more than acquiring materials that are widely held. For example, two good collections on Chicano literature, each with a number of unique titles, may serve both local and national researchers better than one large collection or two collections with a substantial amount of overlap.

In addition to concentrating short-term buying power on a specific area, allocating special project funds may benefit the collections in a number of other ways. Special project funds can be used to fill gaps. Sometimes such gaps in the collections are not considered to be significant or are not even apparent until a new program or a new faculty member appears. But then a library must be able to act quickly and effectively to acquire the needed materials. Every library has gaps, whether from different collecting policies in the past, from lack of funds or lack of attention to particular subject areas. Filling in sets and series, acquiring serial backfiles, completing the works of particular authors—these are collection development goals best accomplished by concentrating funds and efforts for limited periods of time. Moreover, providing funds for special projects may allow the library to cut across the political and institutional constraints on the budget process, and to provide support for interdisciplinary research.

In such cases, the collection goals are specific and finite and the funds needed to achieve these goals should be specific and finite too. The fund from which special projects are supported, however, should be a regular part of the acquisitions budget whenever possible, because the needs are recurrent. New programs and research interests, collection policy changes, new information formats, new gift collections and unique opportunities for acquiring collections continually appear and require new collection development efforts as well as budget allocations.

Special projects allocations are also valuable to bibliographers and collection managers. They encourage the development of bibliographic skills and astute collection evaluation by generating competition for scarce resources.

At the University of Kansas, bibliographers request special project funds in writing as part of the regular budget process. The library's Collection Development Council and its Executive Committee review these requests and recommend which should be funded as well as the total amount of money that should be allocated to a project in any given year. We usually receive requests for two or three times the amount available. Whether or not a request is funded depends on its value to the overall collections but also on the knowledge and skill of the bibliographer making the request. According to Martin this type of budgeting "requires proponents of special proposals to provide evidence to justify an allocation."[6] Bibliographers with a strong knowledge of their subject area and its current literature, of university programs, of faculty and student research, of book dealers and the book trade, and of the library's collection development and budgeting process are more likely to develop good and fundable special project requests.

In the same way, special project funding provides incentives for good collection evaluation practices. Routine checking of standard bibliographies and review articles, close contacts with faculty, experimentation with a variety of evaluation techniques—these may become exciting, regular, and rewarding activities. Bibliographers are bound to be frustrated by time-consuming evaluation projects that produce few if any tangible results for them or for their libraries collections. Special project funding encourages collection evaluation by providing tangible results. Even those bibliographers who do not receive special project funding in a given year are likely to benefit from their increased knowledge of the collections and from the establishment of regular evaluation practices.

In both of these areas, special projects provide opportunities to concentrate and plan for collection growth at an appropriate and manageable level. Most bibliographers deal with subject areas so broad that it is not possible for them to have detailed knowledge about every aspect. Preparing a special project budget request challenges a bibliographer to explore at least a small part of the collections in depth and offers a potential reward for this effort. One of the more psychologically debilitating aspects of a major collection evaluation project is the prospect of being unable to correct any problems revealed. A special project fund allows bibliographers to assess limited parts of the collection, to find the problems and to fix them. The often vague notions of bibliographer responsibility and flexibility are made specific and concrete. Above all, it gives them hope—hope that some of the mistakes of the past and the present may be corrected in the future and hope that their efforts may make a difference and will not slip imperceptibly into a cluttered void. "The Library," may be as Borges says, "unlimited and cyclical."[7] But bibliographers need opportunities to stand aside from the whirl and make specific, limited and measurable contributions.

FLEXIBLE FUNDING

Finally, making special projects a regular part of the acquisitions budget has significant fiscal and collection management implications. In this period of uncertainty about budgets, high inflation rates for library materials, new and expensive formats, and volatile exchange rates, librarians need as much flexibility as possible in the acquisitions budget. Special project funds can easily expand or contract or vanish altogether, without doing permanent damage to the collections. Allocations for other areas such as serials, or current monographs cannot fluctuate much without permanent undesirable effects. Allocations for spe-

Organizing the materials budget to fund special projects for a limited time benefits a collection in a number of ways

. . . providing
funds for special
projects allows
the library to cut
across political
and institutional
constraints on the
budget process

cial projects are always a positive gain for a library. Reducing or eliminating them may be disappointing but it is not crippling in the way that cancelling serials or sharply reducing an approval plan is.

Special project allocations provide flexibility in another way as well. Funded one year at a time, the amount can be re-allocated to other more pressing needs in a particularly tight budget year. This may reduce the need to cancel serials or reduce book funds. At the University of Kansas this has in fact happened. The presence of a sizeable allocation for special projects allocated in 1985–1986 allowed the library to cut its 1986–1987 book budget by three to five percent less than otherwise would have been necessary. Of course once the special projects fund has been eliminated there is no fiscal encore. But the goal is to restore allocations to the budget as soon as possible. In this way the fund doubles as a contingency or reserve fund.

Creating a budget structure that includes continuing provision for special projects is only one way libraries can organize collection development to meet identifiable needs and provide results that can be evaluated. According to Charles Osburn "collection development does seem now to be understood as a process of establishing priorities that will allow the most effective use of a budget in achieving predetermined goals, both long-term and short-term."[8] I think that this modest suggestion represents an effective use of the library's materials budget that will benefit collections and bibliographers. With this method or with another by any other name, librarians interested in their collections will beat on ceaselessly bearing the past into the present so that the appearance of its truths may not be hidden in the future.

References

1. Umberto Eco, The Name of the Rose (New York: Harcourt Brace Jovanovich, 1983), 283.
2. Jorge Luis Borges, "The Library of Babel," in Labyrinths: Selected Stories and other writings (New York: New Directions, 1964), 56.
3. For example, see Peter Sweetman and Paul Wiedemann, "Developing a Library Book-Fund Allocation Formula," Journal of Academic Librarianship, 6 (1980), 268–276 and Gary M. Shirk, "Allocation Formulas for Budgeting Library Materials: Science or Procedure?" Collection Management, 6 (Fall/Winter 1984(, 37–47.
4. Frederick C. Lynden, "Library Materials Budgeting in the Private University Library: Austerity and Action," Advances in Librarianship, 10 (1980), 122.
5. Murray S. Martin, "The Allocation of Money within the Book Budget," in Collection Development in Libraries: A Treatise, eds. Robert D. Stueart and George B. Miller, Jr. (Greenwich, CT.: JAI, 1980), 57.
6. Ibid., 56.
7. Borges, 58.
8. Charles B. Osburn, "Toward a Reconceptualization of Collection Development," in Advances in Library Administration and Organization, 2 (1983), 182.

Cooperative Collection Development Equals Collaborative Interdependence

by Paul H. Mosher

Resource sharing or cooperative collection development among American libraries is not new; history reveals waves of cooperative spirit over many decades. Librarians in the United States—at least since librarianship became a serious professional enterprise around the turn of the century—have exhibited a democratic altruism about information and its distribution that has resulted in the world's richest and most extensive library collections and a tradition of library service unmatched anywhere else on the globe. Cooperative collection development in one guise or another has long been a part of both that spirit and that enterprise.

Ruth Patrick reported in 1971 that at least ten library consortia established between 1931 and 1960 for resource sharing purposes were still operating 11 to 40 years later.[2] By early 1983, two-thirds of the libraries belonging to the Association of Research Libraries were involved in some kind of resource sharing collection development activity.[1] It has become part of the American library tradition.

MYTH OF SELF-SUFFICIENCY

Nevertheless, the spirit of altruism is not always paramount. Each institution's natural desire for academic self-sufficiency helps to foster competition among American university research libraries and a myth of the self-sufficient "comprehensive" collection necessary for any library with pretensions to greatness.

This myth has been punctured by collection overlap studies of libraries of all sizes and types.

Results show that there is a consistently large proportion of unique material distributed among libraries of a region, a state, or even a locality—whatever the mix of libraries: research libraries, multi-type libraries, or small academic libraries with different sets of programs. One surprising discovery was that it is even true of very small libraries in the same locality: in Juneau, Alaska, for example, the Capitol City Consortium of three libraries has only a 15 percent overlap in books, and 24 percent in serials in the field of education (the consortium includes one college, one public, and one state library). Unfortunately, the collections developed randomly rather than through planning, so the three institutions are missing many useful core titles desired by users of all of the institutions. Cooperation would have allowed collaborative development of core or basic collections as well as planned evolution of lesser-used materials, enlarging the pool of resources available to all. The literature describes similar patterns among libraries of all types and sizes in many configurations and in many parts of the country.[3]

REALITY OF COOPERATION

American librarians have come to recognize that circumstances call for cooperation—ways of optimizing service by joining in partnerships or consortia that will allow access to collective resources. Libraries can serve their patrons and programs better, as they become less collection-driven and more client- and program-oriented.

In 1980 the Research Libraries Group (RLG) began a program of mapping the research collections of member libraries using a common frame-

> Libraries can serve their patrons and programs better as they become less collection-driven and more client- and program-oriented

Paul H. Mosher is Director of Libraries at the University of Pennsylvania.

CONCORDIA COLLEGE LIBRARY
BRONXVILLE, N. Y. 10708

work (based on the Library of Congress classification system) and a set of standard codes representing collecting intensities, strength of existing collections, and characteristics of materials collected. This framework, called the *Conspectus,* gives a clearer understanding of collections, collecting efforts, and commitments by participating libraries, and improves local and cooperative collection planning and management options. The *Conspectus* has been adopted by all members of the Association of Research Libraries in the form of the North American Collections Inventory Project (NCIP), and the research libraries of Canada have joined in the effort as well. These new initiatives differ from earlier efforts, such as the Farmington Plan, in their focus on collection development and management rather than blanket acquisition. They are collectively supported by partner libraries rather than depending upon federal subsidies. NCIP and the data contained in its *Conspectus* provide the basis for cooperative efforts in the distribution, cataloging, and preservation of materials as well as for acquisition.

Comparative overlap or "verification" studies of the RLG Conspectus Project show that not even the largest libraries hold all of the significant books in any field of scholarly research. Distribution among libraries forms fascinating—and not always predictable—patterns. Even the Library of Congress with its 14,000,000 volumes, is exceeded by university libraries' holdings in a number of disciplines, such as agricultural economics. In French literature, no library—including the Library of Congress—holds more than 62 percent of the scholarly titles cited. On the other hand, four large university libraries together possessed 83 percent. This data supports Pat Battin's argument that "If we are to acknowledge openly our heretofore implicit acceptance of the responsibility for the health of national scholarship, we must channel our energies into the design and development of effective cooperative activities at the national level, which will then enable us to discharge our obligations to our regional and local colleagues."[4] And these cooperative efforts must involve collaboration and distribution of effort among libraries both within large consortia of research libraries, and among libraries of many types and sizes across the country.

A NEW APPROACH

A new and more useful mythology is called for. We need to go beyond "cooperative" collection development to "collaborative" collection development. Cooperation is the environment needed. The goal, fostered by the atmosphere of cooperation is *collaboration:* working, laboring, thinking, and planning together in new communities of enterprise which transcend the walls of local libraries—or even of large campus library complexes. Collaborative collection development requires communities of librarians who know their patrons and their programs well, and who are active rather than passive in their approach to collections. It requires librarians who act to produce change rather than react to random change.

When we begin to consider collaboration and collection development we enter into a realm seldom mentioned in the literature: the realm of attitudes. Attitudes form the context in which all human activities take place; they are an essential element of culture. In a recent survey of attitudes Hewitt and Shipman found four principal purposes for cooperative collection development programs: "1. To expand the range of research materials available to the community involved in the program. 2. To reduce duplication of expensive research materials. 3. To generally 'coordinate' development of collections and acquisition of materials. 4. To jointly acquire materials."[5]

Other viewpoints expressed in the recent literature also tend to focus on managerially determined outcomes (e.g. the bottom line), with little attention on how to achieve practical results:

- The collections, how inadequate they are and how we can collaborate to do something about it;
- The organizational structure (how should cooperative collection development be organized or structured?)
- The financial aspects (there are inadequate resources to maintain x, y, or z), and
- The "electronic imperative" ("thou shalt network, so shalt thou cooperate").

COOPERATION INVOLVES PEOPLE

Few studies have examined the human dimension of cooperation—collaboration. Few have emphasized the cultural rather than the structural aspects of cooperation, either locally or consortially; few have reflected on the communities of human beings who make the thousands of decisions that generate library collections, the communication between the individuals that form those communities, or the communication between communities that must be at the center of any process of cooperative collection development. Yet it is here— at the human level, and at the basic level of human communication—that cooperative collection development must succeed or fail.

Librarianship is often understood to be an applied social science, or a branch of organizational behavior; so it may be, but it is also a social enterprise, with culture rather than structure at its base, and with communication between humans rather than control by management as its operational routine.

Cooperation is reached by setting common goals rather than working out personal differences or organizational mandates. Cooperation is achieved by working ahead, planning, reflecting, and talking with both users and colleagues about the collections, the programs they serve, and about aspirations for the collections of the future. The accomplishment of a working collaboration among people doing selection and making collection management decisions is more central to effective cooperation within collection development than distribution of subject, language, discipline or format.

If working teams have a common purpose and function, have agreed upon goals and a set of objectives, a time frame, and the means they will use to achieve those goals, effective distribution of responsibility is likely to be a natural outcome along with other functionally desirable outcomes less readily perceived at the outset.

Psychologists' recent studies of cooperation in organizations support the view that effective cooperation is most readily achieved by forming small working teams. Workers should focus on sets of mutually desirable interdependencies and outcomes that link stakeholders, rather than emphasize the issues or problems of a single stakeholder. Such groups tend to foster cooperation rather than competition, and collaboration has been shown to strengthen such groups and encourage them to complete more challenging tasks. Collaboration—working together—on cooperative goals, fosters good work relationships, high morale, productivity and effective group integration.[6] Factors crucial to effective collaboration include: effective mutual communication; helpful attitudes; mutual sensitivity to needs, motives, and concerns; and a cooperative and supportive role by administrators.

Small groups generate more effective communication, shared influence, task orientation, friendliness and support. Studies of group performance have demonstrated that the highest verbal and arithmetical reasoning performance was observed during intergroup cooperation; shared attitudes fostered cooperation. It has also been shown that collaboration in groups engenders greater work-related learning by all participants. Various members of the group know various amounts about subjects discussed. Experts and novices must accommodate their differences, and evaluate, supply, and acquire more knowledge than they would acting independently.[7]

Such studies reveal the significance of the informal and social aspects of collection development and the importance of intergroup learning. They emphasize the benefits of both collaboration and interdependence in cooperative collection development—factors that are important at two levels: that of selectors or bibliographers, and that of the libraries themselves. Protocols, structures and guidelines, the Conspectus and policies, lay the foundation for the collaborative effort necessary to create cooperation, but it is people working in teams, that achieve cooperative collection development goals.

CONOCO STUDY

Since effective collaboration in the collection development sphere is the result of changes in the thousands of individual decisions made by many human beings, it must become habitual and customary to become effective. The potential benefits of collaboration among small groups of individuals were recently demonstrated by the Conoco Study. Members of the Collection Management and Development Committee of RLG (bibliographers from participating institutions and central staff) formed a project team, funded by Conoco, Inc. They surveyed groups of bibliographers from the humanities (German literature) and sciences (Geology) to examine the degree to which cooperative collection development could be effective, and whether goals could be internalized in ways that would affect long-term decision-making.[8] The findings in two areas are particularly relevant here: selector behavior in relation to identified resource sharing goals, and collection overlap.

It was found that German literature selectors were willing to change 40 percent of their selection decisions and rely on collections at other institutions if they could be reasonably sure of both bibliographic access and physical availability of items in those collections (maximum of seven days for delivery of materials). Geology selectors proved willing to change up to 50 percent of their selection decisions, if materials could be secured within three days. Selectors in both the humanities and sciences were more willing to focus cooperative action on materials they considered peripheral. They were reluctant to rely on other collections for materials important to the core of their work— usually curricular, instructional, or basic reference materials. In terms of overlap, the amount and distribution of uniquely held items was both greater and more widely spread than bibliographers had anticipated and, not surprisingly, geology collections proved more homogeneous than

Cooperation is achieved by working ahead, planning, reflecting, and talking with both users and colleagues about the collections, the programs, and aspirations for the collections of the future

German literature collections because of greater dependence on journals.

The results of the Conoco study are heartening. They show the benefit—perhaps the necessity—of personal collaboration in meetings, and team building and team work among bibliographers in realizing benefits of cooperative collection development. The study required collaborative effort among participating bibliographers, who were brought together to carry out the study and design the outcomes as well as prepare to achieve them. It may well be that this is an essential element in developing the collaborative interdependence necessary for effective results in cooperative collection development, and that such activity should be a part of the planning—and funding—for all cooperative collection development ventures.

References

1. Joe A. Hewitt and John S. Shipman, "Cooperative collection development among research libraries in the age of networking," *Advances in Library Automation and Networking,* I (1987), 225.
2. Ruth J. Patrick, *Guidelines for Library Cooperation: Development of Academic Library Consortia.* Santa Monica, 1972.
3. The results of the overlap studies are outlined in Paul H. Mosher, "A National scheme for collaboration in collection development: the RLG-NCIP effort," *Coordinating Cooperative Collection Development: A National Perspective." Resource Sharing and Information Networks,* II(1985) Numbers 3/4, pp. 22–23; and in Mosher, "Quality in library collections: New directions in research and practice in collection evaluation," *Advances in Librarianship,* 13 (1984), 227–230.
4. Patricia N. Battin, "Research libraries in the network environment: the case for cooperation," *Journal of Academic Librarianship,* 6 (1980), 70.
5. Hewitt and Shipman, 207.
6. (See, for example, Dean Tjosvold, "Cooperation theory and organizations," *Human Relations,* 37 (1984), 743–67; Barbara Gray, "Conditions facilitating interorganizational collaboration," *Human Relations,* 38 (1985), 911–36: Donald T. Tuler, "Professor-practitioner collaboration: an analysis of factors enhancing collaboration in education," (PhD dissertation, University of Wisconsin, Madison, 1983.) *Dissertation Abstracts International* Volume 44, No. 3, p. 640A.
7. Ellen A. Issacs, and Herbert H. Clark, "References in conversation between experts and novices," *Journal of Experimental Psychology: General,* 116 (1987), 26–37; Rupert Brown and Domino Adams "The effects of intergroup similarity and goal interdependence on intergroup attitudes and task performance," *Journal of Experimental Social Psychology,* 22 (1986), 78–92.
8. "Conoco Project: Executive Summary". An unpublished report. The Research Libraries Group, Stanford, Calif., May 13, 1987. Participating institutions in German were Columbia, Brigham Young, Cornell, N.Y.P.L., Stanford, Northwestern, Penn, Minnesota and Yale. Those in Geology were Colorado State, Columbia, Iowa, Minnesota, Stanton, N.Y.P.C. and Suny Stony Brook.
9. "Conoco Project: Executive Summary," pp. i–iv.

Collection Evaluation in the Research Library

by Ferne B. Hyman

Among many unflattering characterizations of librarians is the one that accuses us of wishing to keep *our* collections neat, clean and in proper order on the shelves. That is, not being used. This is a half-true, if exaggerated, statement. As rational professionals, librarians realize that if a collection is well used it is not always in order and available, or else the collection is not as good as it should be. Control—knowing where an item is, who has it—is the goal librarians strive to achieve, rather than maintaining every item in its place.

Knowing the "where" and "who" of the collection is important, but knowing "what" is in the collection and whether it meets the objectives and goals of the institution the library serves is equally important. Evaluating holdings is necessary to ensure that a library is providing useful materials.

The Chronicle of Higher Education reported in August, 1986, that scholars in the humanities and social sciences "have strongly criticized some of the mainstays of their professions—including . . . the availability of research material in college and university libraries."[1] The article continues, "nearly half rate the book collections in their institutions' libraries only fair or poor in meeting their research needs. About one-third make similar evaluations of their libraries' journal collection, as about one-fourth do of newspapers and other references sources."

If half of the college and university faculty rate library collections as only fair to poor it follows that librarians must work toward improving their collections to better serve one of their primary constituents. Regularly evaluating collections is one of the major means of establishing the value of materials to specific users.

In a recent article criticizing the *Chronicle's* reporting of the survey, that publication was faulted for ignoring many of the survey's less negative conclusions.[2] Even so, the least laudatory statements indicate that librarians need to do a better job communicating information about available research and instructional support. Faculty who are unaware of library holdings are certainly not served by the library; it is not surprising that they should criticize the library's collections.

The locus of responsibility and the methods used to collect materials have changed over the years. In the past, faculty of colleges and universities assumed the major responsibility for book selection. Librarians took over much of the selection chores when expansion of university programs and the building of library collections reached a high point during the 1960s. As research in librarianship shows, both the campus programs and library support went beyond traditional acquisitions to the purchasing of large research collections.[3] In the late 1960s and early 1970s when the great expansion was curtailed, librarians continued to develop collections rather than revert to faculty selection.

As collection development became the new approach, the literature on the subject expanded and methods of evaluating collections were discussed. In 1979 the Collections Development Committee of the Resources and Technical Services Division within the American Library Association produced the *Guidelines for Collection Development*.[4] These guidelines were concerned with formulating written collection development policies and the "Evaluations of the Effectiveness of Library Collections." The guidelines included a list of purposes: "research, recreation, community service and development, instruction, support of a

> . . . librarians need to do a better job communicating information about available research and instructional support

---

Ferne B. Hyman is Assistant University Librarian for Collections Management at Rice University.

corporate activity, or a combination of these." Evaluation is a process to determine whether or not the collection meets the objectives and how well it serves users. The guidelines called for more objectivity in evaluation.[5] In making recommendations, the committee relied largely upon publications that still remain valuable standards today: George S. Bonn's article, "Evaluation of the Collection," and F.W. Lancaster's Book, *Measurement and Evaluation of Library Services*.[6] Paul Mosher's compilation of the literature on collection evaluation from earlier decades is another source.[7] Blaine Hall produced a manual for collection evaluation that detailed methodology and suggested answers to specific evaluative questions.[8]

CHOOSING A METHOD

Library administrators must join collection development librarians in choosing the best approach to evaluating their collections. Various costs, including staff time, can make a complete evaluation prohibitively expensive. The first step is deciding which section of the collection to evaluate. Which disciplines are expanding or contracting and how fast; where are budgets consistently inappropriate; in which departments are faculty and students most critical of the library? The answers to these questions will point to areas which cry out for evaluation. Next, a choice must be made between collection-centered or people-centered studies. Qualitative and/or quantitative approaches may be employed.

Collection Centered

A collection-centered study involves counting the number of volumes owned and comparing the numbers with libraries in universities offering comparable programs. The numbers may be checked against minimum standards set by accrediting and other educational agencies. Conventional wisdom is that numbers correlate with excellence: the larger the numbers, the greater the chance of having items users need. Another collection-centered approached is to check, the holding against bibliographic lists from different sources. Lists might include catalogs of published titles considered standard works, extensive bibliographies in a particular subject, specialized lists, as well as shelf lists from other established collections. An advantage of collection-centered approaches is that they provide a firm grasp of both quantitative and qualitative comparative information. The disadvantage is that programs and activities of other institutions, though similar, are not identical— particularly in the area of faculty research. Numbers compared and titles listed do not necessarily address the question of users' needs.

User Centered

User-centered studies are more subjective and intuitive. They should be included in an evaluation, but the results will be suggestive rather than definitive. One user-centered method, evaluating circulation statistics, counts which titles are used and, with computerized data, who uses them. These numbers reveal how often some items are used and which are currently vital for instruction, but they do not show which titles have been or will become important for research or instruction. Nor can in-house use be fully established. In some studies in-house and circulation records are similar enough to be used, while other studies do not show a correlation.

Asking users for information on how often and how well a library responds to their needs, gives swift feedback. One important factor in user satisfaction is access: not only ownership of a title, but availability on the shelves. Therefore, evaluation should follow-through to determine accessibility.[9] A successful interlibrary loan program can improve user satisfaction by securing needed titles in a timely manner.

The citation study is one means of evaluating acquisition of journal titles. By checking standard citations indexes, librarians can point to the journals most frequently cited by authors who are publishing in the various fields studied.[10] This is helpful in assessing the value of in-house titles, and deciding which titles to purchase or prune.

The advantages and disadvantages of these collection evaluation techniques are well covered in the literature. In general, they are most useful for evaluating holdings for instructional support, but are not as valuable when assessing research support. Additional evaluation measures are required to assess collections in this area.

DOING RESEARCH

The university has become a vital center for expanding research projects since World War II. Federal government funding, as well as enlarged private foundation support, has accelerated research activity in all disciplines. Universities enrollments expanded, bringing increasing numbers of faculty and projects. The publish or perish environment on the campus has continued to fuel the explosion in research projects. Jacques Barzun, in a recent article, suggests that the academy has, perhaps, gone too far and that it is time to take a long look at "doing research":

The best means of rescuing research in the long run is the steady encouragement of solid, manifestly useful undertakings. In the modern infatuation with "findings" these are at a disadvantage: they look regular, not innovative; they call for sober work, not fancy techniques; they promise utility along recognized lines, not amazing revelations and upside-down revisionism. With common sense in charge, the superstitious regard for "doing research" could be held in check, if not dispelled, and the genuine investigation of great subjects might once more give to research and its products the value and the praise they used to deserve.[11]

The library is affected by the "doing research" frenzy Barzun mentions. Cooperation between researchers and librarians is essential for "encouragement of solid . . . undertakings."

Charles Osburn comments in his study of changing patterns of academic research that the research enterprise between the library and the university community does not function as a system. Library resources are not an immediate part of research fund requests either from federal or private sources. Library materials are often included in overhead figures at the last minute for large grant requests, causing the libraries to react and try to support research rather than having the opportunity for planning in advance with the faculty for the specific project.[12] Libraries are largely unprepared for expanding and changing research techniques. New technologies add to the problems facing librarians.

EXPLORING INNER SPACE

Space is a prominent and persistent problem. During the great expansion of the 1960s, many new facilities appeared but collection requirements outgrew the facilities, and they continue to do so. There was a stabilization of financial support in the 1970s,[13] but the programs and the continued need to support research put strains on available space and budgets. The need for discrimination became evident. Through collection evaluation, librarians have been able to take a more selective approach to collection development, not only to support instruction, but also to support graduate and faculty research.

No one disputes the fact that the cost to support a major research collection is greater than to sustain an undergraduate program. A 1966 study by E.W. Reichard and T. J. Orsagh ". . . noted growth in collection size and expenditures correlated with faculty growth and expansion of graduate programs; [but found] no ascertainable correlation with growth in undergraduate population."[14] It is, therefore, important for librarians to be aware

of planned new graduate programs in order to assess library support. New faculty appointments should also be routinely reported in advance so that collections may be evaluated to determine whether they will accommodate new research interests. In a *New York Times* column about the American Council of Learned Societies survey, Fred Hechinger quotes scholars finding inadequate resources for research in libraries.[15] With space and cost reductions, librarians have to find out whether their collections are adequate for faculty research programs. The budgetary implications for libraries and the impact on faculty careers are too significant to ignore. Libraries provide the knowledge and information needed to further man's understanding and fuel technological innovation.

SHARING COLLECTIONS

In 1974, the Research Libraries Group (RLG) was formed by the chief collection development librarians of Columbia, Yale, New York Public, and Harvard. This cooperative group was created to alleviate some of the problems of rapid expansion. Its members have changed over the years, as it has grown. Now a computer-based bibliographic processing system, RLIN, is used to expedite its cooperative plans.

John Finzi of the Library of Congress presented a paper at the ALA Annual Conference in 1978 suggesting a distribution of collection responsibilities among institutions. His reasoning was that no one library, not even the Library of Congress, could collect in all areas to suit all users.[16] Out of that beginning, the chief collection development officers of institutions from the Research Libraries Group moved forward to establish the RLG Conspectus.

As Guinn and Mosher reported, "the Conspectus is an overview, or summary of existing strengths and future collecting intensities of RLG members."[17] The planners of the Conspectus have encouraged other libraries to subscribe to provide a national cooperative collection development effort. The Conspectus is a long-term effort for cooperating libraries to inventory their collections and to develop institutional policies to support individual and local needs and programs. Cooperating libraries agree to serve as collectors of record for specific, often narrow, subject areas. Access is provided to research material, if not ownership of the titles.

The labor of inventorying collections has been justified by recognition of the need for cooperative effort. The Conspectus is broken down into Library of Congress classification schedules to permit ap-

One user-centered method, evaluating circulation statistics, counts which titles are used and, with computerized data, who uses them

Libraries are
largely
unprepared for
expanding and
changing research
techniques. New
technologies add
to the problem

proaching both inventory and collecting responsibilities in workable segments.

Participating libraries have collection development policies to fit local situations, and through the RLG Shared Resources Programs, knowledge of research materials among members. Many libraries in the Association of Research Libraries are participating in an ARL/RLG project, the North American Collection Inventory Project (NCIP), which is an attempt to inventory collections outside the original group. Funding support for this project is from the Council on Library Resources, the Lilly Endowment and the Andrew Mellon Foundation. As reported in *American Libraries,* "[t]he project is meant to strengthen coordinated management of national research collections and help determine shared responsibilities for the resources."[18] The potential benefits as outlined in the ARL proposal are:

1. Availability of a standard tool for collection description and assessment for the identification of North American collection strengths and weaknesses;
2. Development of a mechanism to locate needed research materials more expeditiously;
3. Development of the capacity to relate local collection development policies to collection levels at other institutions and to serve as the basis for cooperative collection development, both nationally and regionally;
4. Development of the capacity to relate collection development strengths to cataloging and preservation needs and to serve as the basis for cooperative cataloging and preservation efforts, again both nationally and regionally;
5. Support for emerging coordinated retrospective conversion projects; and
6. Enhancement of individual libraries' collection management programs. Analysis of Conspectus data will lead to identification of collection strengths and weaknesses, contribute to the preparation of collection development policies, and to improve budget allocation decisions.[19]

Scholars are the final arbiters of what the library must contain to support research. However, without librarians, they have less chance of finding appropriate holdings in any collection. The complaints of researchers about the quantity and quality of library holdings are compounded by the problem of keeping up with growing numbers of publications in most disciplines. Worse, some are of questionable value. Recent scandals caused by falsified reports or premature release of unproven research results, serve to warn both scholars and librarians of the need to evaluate individual titles. The paradox of too much and not enough is hard on the scholar and the librarian.[20]

Evaluation is mostly hindsight. As Oscar Handlin, the Harvard historian/librarian, wrote: "Building collections to satisfy current demands is building them too late, and librarians must anticipate research interests of twenty years hence."[21] A challenge, indeed. In order to make decisions about the future, librarians must work in the present, and study what was needed in the past. Close ties between faculty and librarians are essential to future planning. Techniques specifically for evaluating research materials and researchers' satisfaction levels will help the library find out whether it has successfully supported current research projects.

In 1983, librarians at the University of California at Irvine conducted an "investigation of collection support for doctoral research" on their campuses. They focused on graduate students' requirements for doctoral research. Their method was to examine a sample of bibliographies in dissertations completed at the University against the holdings of the library. The results confirmed that the library had a large portion of the secondary materials required by those users. Nuances within that assessment, however, showed areas that needed additional attention for collection building.

The faculty and students are being well served if the library is able to supply a significant portion of required titles either in-house or through interlibrary loans. If most of the works have been obtained by the faculty without recourse to library facilities, then improvements should be made in the support of research.

Checking bibliographies of published faculty research as well as graduate dissertations broadens the evaluation base. Verifying shelf availability of titles is essential to be sure they are not lost from the collection. At the same time, evaluating the condition of materials can aid preservation/conservation activity.

Recent emphasis on bibliographic instruction, including working with students and faculty on new technologies to enhance research has produced less than spectacular results so far. Some faculty still prefer informal research networks, the so-called "invisible college," to library facilities or librarians' help. It seems easier to telephone a colleague for information than to work through the library/index system and perhaps still not find the title needed. This attitude is gradually changing as technology for database searching becomes more available and sophisticated. CD-ROMs and advancements in other technologies, impress even the reluctant, cautious users.

Planning for these new tools and technologies is essential. Resources are limited and faculty requirements often know no bounds. Knowing what materials are available where they are and who is and will be using them, gives librarians confidence to meet users' demands.

Basic research-centered evaluation techniques are a good way to assess how well the library serves the researcher/user. Quantitative reports from automated circulation and acquisitions systems and the results of the NCIP studies, give librarians the information they need to become effective research colleagues in the academic world. By embracing this labor-intensive work, librarians can strengthen working relationships with faculty. Evaluation enables collection managers to do a better job of developing collections and supplying information needed for the research university library's primary user group—faculty and researchers.

References

1. Jacobson, Robert L., "Scholars Fault Journals and College Libraries in Survey by Council of Learned Societies," *Chronicle of Higher Education,* 33 April 6, 1986, 181.

2. Epp, Ronald, H. and Segal, JoAnn, "The ACLS Survey and Academic Library Service" in *College and Research Libraries News,* 48 (2) February, 1987, 63–69.

3. Bonk, Wallace J. and Magrill, Rose Mary, *Building Library Collections,* N.Y., Scarecrow Press, 1979, 26.

4. American Library Association, *Guidelines for Collection Development,* Chicago, American Library Association, 1979.

5. Ibid, 9.

6. Bonn, George S., "Evaluation of the Collection" Library Trends, 22 (3) (January 1974), 265–304.

7. Lancaster, F.W., *Measurement and Evaluation of Library Services,* Washington, Information Resources Press, 1977.

8. Mosher, Paul H. "Collection Evaluation in Research Libraries: the Search for Quality, Consisten-cy and System in Collecting Development" *Library Resources and Technical Services,* 23 Winter, 1979; 16–32.

9. Hall, Blaine H., *Collection Assessment Manual for College and University Libraries,* Phoenix, Ariz., Oryx Press, 1985.

10. Discussed in Magrill, Rose Mary, "Evaluation by Library Type" *Library Trends,* 33 Winter, 1985, 281.

11. An excellent overview of methods of evaluations in Mosher, Paul H., "Collection Evaluation or Analysis: Matching Library Acquisitions to Library Needs" in Stueart, Robert D. and Miller, George B. Jr., *Collection Development in Libraries: A Treatise,* Greenwich, Conn., JA Press v12, 527–545.

12. Barzun, Jacques, "Doing Research—Should the Sport be Regulated?" *Columbia,* February, 1987, 22.

13. Osburn, Charles B., *Academic Research and Library Resources: Changing Patterns in American,* Westport, Conn., Greenwood Press 1979, 144.

14. Bonk and Magrill, *Building Library Collections,* 26.

15. As quoted in Lancaster, *Measurement and Evaluation of Library Service,* 172.

16. Hechinger, Fred "About Education" *New York Times,* Sept. 30, 1986, 21–22.

17. Described in the article by Gwinn, Nancy E. and Mosher, Paul H., "Coordinating Collection Development: the RLG Conspectus" in *College and Research Libraries,"* 44 March 1983, 128–144.

18. Guinn and Mosher, "Coordinating Collection Development the RLG Conspectus," 129.

19. "In Support of Scholarly Research," *American Libraries,* March 18, 1987, 188.

20. Quoted in Sohn, Jeanne, "Cooperative Collection Development: A Brief Overlay" *Collection Management,* 8 (2) Summer 1986, 7.

21. An example is in the *Chronicle of Higher Education* for December 31, 1986.

22. Handlin, Oscar "Research Library Collection" *College and Research Libraries* May, 1984, 217.

23. Buzzard, Marion L. and New, Doris E. "An Investigation of Collection Support for Doctoral Research," *College and Research Libraries,* 44 Nov. 1983, 469–475.

Preservation and Collection Management: Some Common Concerns

by Margaret M. Byrnes

Awareness of the integral and necessary relationship between collection management and development and preservation programs has been increasing in recent years. At long last, collection managers and preservation specialists have begun to work together more closely and to identify areas of common concern.

Changes in the organization of library operations are being made, because the connection between collection management and development and preservation programs is more widely understood. In the past, many institutions limited collection development to fund allocation and the selection of new materials. If selectors had any involvement in preservation activities, it was usually only decisions to replace deteriorated materials. Often preservation was regarded as a separate function, mainly book repair and binding. Today it is part of the Collection Management and Development Office and its functions have been integrated with other collection management activities. As selectors' roles have gradually been broadened to include collection evaluation, storage, weeding, and treatment decisions, frequent interaction with preservation staff is necessary. Furthermore, there is new emphasis on maintaining fragile retrospective collections because the high cost of not doing so is now recognized. Temperature and humidity controls, and careful attention to commercial binding methods and materials are essential ingredients of collection management programs.

The relationship between preservation and collection development is obvious in libraries that fund at least some preservation activities from the materials budget; selectors are responsible for administering funds intended for both acquisitions of new materials and replacement of deteriorated titles. Issues related to budget are probably the most important area of common concern. Budgets are seldom large enough to buy everything needed for a collection. Consequently, a healthy tension tends to develop between the need to acquire new materials and the need to maintain what has already been acquired.

Replacement decisionmaking is arguably a form of second selection. Just as no library can afford to buy everything published, no library can hope to replace all of its brittle books. Many of the criteria used in replacement decisionmaking are similar to those used in selection of new materials (e.g., significance of author or edition, relationship of the subject to collection strengths and current research activity, probable demand, availability elsewhere, and cost). Areas of mutual interest include the role of faculty in decisionmaking, user preferences in choice of format, the need to balance both current demand and future needs, local priorities and regional or national collecting obligations, and the impact of new publishing technologies.

The recent literature in both fields reflects a widespread desire to develop viable resource sharing programs. Costs of an increasing volume of important research materials published each year continue to exceed any one institution's ability to acquire all of them. Research libraries must rely more on cooperative acquisitions agreements for less frequently used materials. Within the Research Libraries Group, the assignment of subjects of primary collecting responsibility (PCRs) and

> **Preservation must be dramatically increased if we are not to lose a substantial portion of the late nineteenth and early twentieth century imprints held by American research libraries**

Margaret M. Byrnes is Head of the Preservation Section of the National Library of Medicine.

current discussion concerning the desirability of assigning subjects of primary preservation responsibility (PPRs) reflect this trend. For collection managers and preservation specialists alike, such agreements raise difficult issues of access and ownership. They also highlight the close interrelationship between the two fields.

BUDGET IMPACT

In moments of despair over the potential costs, several library directors have been heard to refer to preservation as a "black hole." This is quite understandable when one considers the statistics. In at least one of the country's older research libraries, 37 percent of the collection is dangerously brittle and the total proportion of acidic bookpaper is as high as 83 percent. The Library of Congress estimates that approximately 77,000 volumes in that collection become brittle each year. Another study shows the median cost of preservation microfilming (including all stages from identifying an item to providing a bibliographic record for and storing the completed film) is approximately $50 per volume. Guidelines issued by the Association of Research Libraries call for a minimum of 10 percent of ARL members' materials budgets or four percent of their current operating funds to be devoted to preservation programs. It is clear that many libraries are unable to begin to meet that minimum standard. It is also clear that preservation activity throughout the country must be dramatically increased if we are not to lose a substantial portion of the late nineteenth and early twentieth century imprints held by American research libraries.

Considering the size of the problem and the cost of attempting to solve it, it is hardly surprising that preservation programs are straining most library budgets. It is hard to budget for replacement of deteriorated materials when under pressure to buy more current monographs and pay the increasing costs of serials subscriptions. Selectors are often reluctant to use their limited funds for replacement of older materials that may or may not be needed for future research.

The practice of combining funds for preservation with those for acquisition of new materials has some merit; it makes the selector more directly responsible for the retrospective collection. The need to provide funds for preservation replacements will vary according to the age and condition of different parts of the collection, the amount of use they have received, and research patterns typical of each discipline. In addition, the availability of commercial replacements (whether reprints or microforms) varies considerably among subjects. Another critical factor is the amount of time each selector can devote to preservation decisionmaking. Establishing a single replacement fund to be used as needs are identified and opportunities arise can reduce the natural tension between the need to purchase new materials and the need to replace the old; it can also result in a more efficient use of funds and personnel and a net increase in the number of preservation replacements acquired each year.

Many of the libraries which have established new preservation programs in recent years have done so primarily with funds obtained by means of internal reallocation and grants from outside sources. Some of the largest preservation programs in the country have been developed without any permanent budget increases from parent institutions. While they provide a model of resourcefulness and creative budgeting, many have reached their limits in terms of finding new ways to allocate existing monies.

Relying upon grants as a source of program support is inadvisable as it exacerbates the difficulty of maintaining existing operations and planning for needed expansion of preservation activities. Projects funded by grants often do not reflect an institution's top preservation priorities and continuing existing projects or initiating new ones is almost always uncertain. In addition, grant funding is difficult to obtain for costly but essential preventive preservation measures such as security systems and air conditioning and humidity control for stack areas. Use of the materials budget for these measures, or for protective enclosures and nondamaging processing and storage supplies is rarely approved, despite the fact that replacement and repair programs are ineffective unless basic preventive measures are in place.

Results of current research in mass deacidification, paper strengthening, and optical disk technology will affect long term preservation budget planning. If these techniques look feasible and desirable, sources for large amounts of additional funding will have to be found.

University administrators and state legislators must become more aware of preservation needs and costs if libraries are to fund preservation programs adequately. In most cases, this will require a major shift in priorities on the part of budget officers in research libraries' parent institutions and members of state and federal appropriations committees. It is essential that library directors and preservation experts work together to communicate their current and projected preservation needs and to obtain adequate resources to address those needs.

Results of current research in mass deacidification, paper strengthening, and optical disk technology will affect long term preservation budget planning

NATIONAL PRESERVATION PLANNING

The Council on Library Resources' has established a Commission on Preservation and Access to inform legislators and the general public of the magnitude of the preservation problem. There are an estimated 75 million brittle books in American research libraries. To preserve only three million volumes will cost approximately $200 million over the next 10 to 15 years. Figures such as these make it clear that the only hope of accomplishing even a portion of the needed work will be through cooperative preservation activities. Fortunately, a number of recent microfilming projects such as those of the Research Libraries Group, the American Theological Library Association and the American Philological Association have demonstrated that well planned cooperative efforts can be successful. There is, however, a critical need to secure major new funding if efforts are to reach an adequate level.

Selection of materials for inclusion in the national brittle book program is now a topic of fairly intense discussion. Earlier cooperative microfilming projects included item by item review by selectors or faculty members to ensure that only the most important materials would be filmed. Because it is hoped that the national brittle book program will increase the current level of preservation activities by tenfold the wisdom of attempting to decide what will or will not be of research interest in future years is being questioned. Strong arguments are being made for the comprehensive preservation of major subject collections at institutions which have been collecting in a specific discipline at the research level for many years. If funding permits, a second sweep would be conducted by another research library with an equally strong ranking in that subject to ensure that important titles were not missed. Assuming that such an approach is affordable, a number of important issues remain to be addressed:

Choice of Collections

Is the wholesale preservation of distinguished collections appropriate for all disciplines? Such an approach may be justifiable in the humanities, but not in the sciences and technology. While title by title review by selectors or other subject specialists is admittedly expensive, it is still necessary for some disciplines to avoid wasting limited funds on materials of little historical value.

Local vs. National Priorities

In most local preservation programs, materials are identified for treatment or replacement as they are returned from circulation. This method meets immediate needs and avoids the political problems inherent in policy decisions to preserve materials in some disciplines rather than others. Nevertheless, the most important or most endangered parts of the collection may not get needed attention and future research may be compromised.

As the national brittle book program evolves, libraries and their primary users will have to balance local and national priorities. If the program is to succeed, libraries with significant subject collections will be obligated to preserve those materials for the rest of the library community. Since full funding is unlikely to be available for national program participants, library staff will need to work hard to convince local users and budget administrators of the long-term local benefit of this approach.

Format Preferences

How should institutions planning to participate in the national brittle book program respond to user preference for paper copy? While making photocopies may be desirable from the user's point of view, many preservation experts do not consider it appropriate for a national cooperative program. They argue that most libraries can afford to produce only one photocopy before discarding the original, thereby risking total loss of information if the photocopy is lost, mutilated, or damaged by water or fire. Photocopying does not lend itself to producing additional copies as needed by other libraries to replace their brittle volumes since a photocopy of a photocopy generally is not very legible. By contrast, future availability of the information and ease of duplication are ensured in properly conducted preservation microfilming programs since they include the production of master negatives (which, when processed correctly and stored under archival conditions, are expected to last many hundreds of years). These master negatives can then be used to produce reading copies requested by other libraries. Photocopying might be an acceptable preservation measure if multiple copies were made and stored in separate locations. A preferable solution is to film the materials first and then photocopy the originals or produce paper copies from the film. Such an expensive process should be limited to frequently used items or those with illustrations that will not reproduce adequately on microfilm.

Microfilm, it must be admitted, is not the format

of choice for most users. However, until further research has been completed for newer technologies that are potentially less cumbersome (e.g., optical digital disk systems) and they are shown to be both feasible and affordable for collection preservation purposes, microfilm will remain the best solution. Barring the unexpectedly rapid development of alternative technologies, many major subject collections will be converted to film during the next decade. Libraries should be hard at work educating their users about preservation so they may begin to understand that microfilm provides access to information that otherwise would no longer be available.

Access to Preserved Materials

Most libraries will not be able to purchase microfilm copies of all collections filmed under the national brittle book program. More than ever before, their users will have to rely on access to materials owned by other institutions. How should libraries begin to prepare their users for this eventuality? Much remains to be done to inform users about the need for a national brittle book program and to develop a broad perspective on issues of access and ownership. A recent study of selection practices shows that providing remote access to lower use materials may not be as controversial as was once feared, if delivery of those materials is reasonably fast. While efforts are being made to improve the efficiency of interlibrary loan services, other possibilities such as increased use of telefacsimile should be explored. If the national brittle book program is to succeed, prompt access to materials must be a critical component in planning for cooperative preservation activities.

Collection Ratings

Implicit in the national brittle book program is the premise that materials will be preserved only once. If a major subject collection has been preserved by one library, others can discard their original copies when they become too deteriorated for use. What are the implications for current standards of collection evaluation? Reliance on collection size as a major indicator of institutional ranking may become invalid. What will be important is the degree to which libraries are able to provide immediate access to high-demand materials and prompt retrieval from other institutions of less frequently used items.

Faculty and Selector Involvement

The role that faculty members, selectors, and scholarly associations should play in national brittle book program decision making remains to be defined. Assistance in identifying those distinctive collections which should be preserved for the nation will clearly be needed. Also useful will be advice concerning which disciplines do not warrant wholesale preservation. Inviting groups of scholars and bibliographers to develop general guidelines and priorities for selecting materials to be preserved is probably the most practical way to take advantage of needed expertise without unduly imposing on busy work schedules. The conclusion being reached by many who have had experience with other preservation projects is that the large scale of the national brittle book program will probably preclude title by title review.

Collection Assessment

Several studies in recent years have shown that the amount of duplication of titles held by research libraries is not as high as previously thought. There is, therefore, a significant risk that a number of important materials will not be preserved because they were not held in the designated preservation collection of record. The study findings lend credence to the argument that second sweep projects will be essential; they also serve to emphasize the importance of documenting collection strengths and weaknesses through collection assessment and overlap studies. Subject bibliographers and collection managers will be greatly needed to conduct such studies and to contribute their knowledge of the collections to national brittle book program planning so that all important materials eventually are preserved.

Copyright

Nagging questions surrounding copyright restrictions remain unresolved. It seems clear that libraries are free to create reproductions of their own holdings for the purpose of replacing deteriorated materials that are no longer available from publishers. Supplying copies of those reproductions to other institutions for the same purpose is, however, very much in question if they might still be protected by copyright. The need to acquire copyright clearance or permission from the publisher before purchasing microfilm copies of thousands of deteriorated titles published within the past 75 years would be a heavy burden for most libraries. Another problem is distinguishing between preservation replacement copies and those sold for the purposes of collection development. This is a particular problem for serials since libraries request copies of substantial runs on microfilm for the dual purpose of replacing deteriorated holdings and filling in missing volumes. Before the national brittle book program can become truly operational, such questions must be addressed.

Bibliographic Access

Access to records of titles preserved as a result of local preservation programs or as part of the national brittle book program must be easily available. Fortunately, notable progress in this area has already been made: OCLC and RLIN have begun to regularly exchange and load tapes of microfilm records contributed by their members; use of the 583 field in the USMARC format was recently approved for recording detailed preservation information; and titles to be included in preservation projects can now be identified with the help of a shadow file in RLIN which contains records from retrospective conversion projects. Use of this file to identify older materials in need of preservation seems a very sensible approach. In future years there will be little point to having bibliographic access to these materials if they are too deteriorated for use. Efforts should continue to encourage:

- the development of a queuing feature in OCLC (i.e., the ability to indicate the intention to film a specific title)
- the exchange of queued records among the major utilities
- more creative uses of automated records to identify collections of importance
- ways to equably allocate preservation responsibilities among the country's research libraries.

It is imperative that information on what has been filmed and what is being filmed is easily and promptly available if costly duplication of effort is to be avoided.

Sources of Funding

The National Endowment for the Humanities, the Council on Library Resources, the Association of Research Libraries, and the Andrew Mellon Foundation, among others, have contributed generously to preservation efforts over the years. The state legislatures of New York and California have provided good examples to the rest of the country by providing substantial support for library preservation programs. In early 1987 a congressional hearing on brittle books raised hopes for increased

federal support. It was held by Representative Pat Williams, chairman of the House Committee on Education and Labor's Subcommittee on Postsecondary Education. Much more lobbying on the federal level remains to be done, however.

Financial commitment from many more institutions and foundations will be required for a successful national program. Libraries without preservation programs or significant brittle book problems must recognize their obligation to share the financial burden. Preserving the country's research materials will ultimately benefit all future users. While only a small number of research libraries may actually preserve materials as part of the national program, many libraries must support the effort.

International Preservation Efforts

Coordination with preservation programs in foreign countries is essential, since American libraries alone cannot afford to preserve all endangered published materials. A program of cooperative planning is needed as well as a system for communicating what is being preserved.

Recently, there have been a number of promising developments. A core program in conservation has been established by the International Federation of Library Associations, headquartered at the Library of Congress. In addition, a few foreign libraries have begun to search the OCLC and RLIN databases for cataloging data and now have access to hundreds of thousands of records of microforms produced in the U.S. The decision by the British Library to load records into RLIN from its Eighteenth Century Short Title Catalog project opens the door to future sharing of bibliographic information produced by that major institution. Plans are under way for national registers of microform masters in the UK, France, and Italy and a feasibility study has been done for a European register. Nonetheless, many difficulties must be overcome in coordinating preservation efforts on the international level, if we are to minimize costly duplication of effort and the risk of losing hundreds of thousands of important research materials.

NEW FORMATS

Magnetic Tape and Disk

In the future, collection managers will find themselves faced with more selection decisions for materials produced in new formats such as CD-ROM, subscriptions to serials published in online form, and information available to researchers only on computer tapes. Preservation specialists must be increasingly concerned with these formats and the longevity of the information they

To preserve only three million of the estimated 75 million brittle books in U.S. research libraries will cost approximately $200 million over the next 10 to 15 years

contain. Research data available only in electronic form will be one of the future's major preservation challenges, particularly for information in science and technology.

The preservation of data stored on magnetic media is an infant field. At present, most information on tape or disk is not intended for permanent retention. For electronic information of more lasting value, some guidelines are available on optimum storage conditions and the frequency with which tapes and diskettes should be copied. However, detailed information on electronic media longevity is sparse, possibly because of the proprietary nature of the results of laboratory studies conducted by the private sector. Longevity can of course be increased by transferring data to computer output microform (COM) which, if produced and stored according to archival standards, should have the same lifespan as any other preservation microfilm. Work is being done on the use of scanners to convert COM data back into a form that can be manipulated on whatever new hardware is available at the time the information is needed. While COM may be one solution to the long term storage of computer data, the advantages and disadvantages of microforms still apply.

Optical Digital Disk Technology

During the past two years, there has been a noticeable increase in the number of titles available in CD-ROM or other optical digital disk formats. Some libraries are beginning to purchase them as a matter of course. To date, however, little thought has been given to the longevity of the data being acquired. As long as information issued in this format is rapidly superseded or of only temporary reference value, image permanence is not of particular concern. However, it is likely that many more titles will appear in CD-ROM or some similar form during the next decade. The question of longevity must soon be addressed by those who acquire such materials for their collections and those responsible for preserving them.

While some longevity studies have been conducted by the Library of Congress, the National Bureau of Standards, and optical disk producers, little information is available in the literature. Estimates of the lifespan of digital data stored on optical disk range from ten to thirty years, depending upon the manufacturer. Fortunately, this is not as critical an issue as it is for other media such as microforms or analog videodiscs, since digital signals can be restored to their original form after the disk deteriorates. What is important for the future, however, is the cost involved in the periodic reading and regeneration of digital disks. Whether

libraries will have the resources for this type of preservation activity remains a major question.

Using optical digital disk technology to preserve information in brittle books and other deteriorated library materials is a strong future possibility. Features which could make it a very attractive alternative to microforms include: extremely condensed data storage; the capacity for image enhancement and more accurate display of graphic material; resistance to wear and tear; and greatly increased ease of access since the images can be linked electronically to citations in bibliographic databases. In addition, because computer networks can be used to provide rapid access to information stored at other locations, optical disk technology may offer solutions to several of the problems associated with cooperative preservation and resource sharing programs.

The feasibility of using optical disk as a preservation medium is being examined in pilot projects at the Library of Congress and the National Archives and Records Administration, and in research under way at the National Library of Medicine. NLM's research and development activities should yield much useful information about document conversion rates, image quality, optimum workflow configurations, quality control strategies, and costs. If it demonstrates that conversion can be accomplished in an efficient and affordable manner and if disk formats and equipment are standardized within the next several years, optical digital disk technology may begin to play a major role in library preservation programs.

Assuming that costs will not be insignificant and that libraries will not have the resources to convert all deteriorated materials, several important questions will need to be addressed in the near future:

- Is the cost of using advanced technology warranted for older materials that receive relatively little use?
- If some materials continue to be microfilmed, what criteria will be used to decide which titles or subjects will be converted to disk and which will be filmed?
- Is conversion of deteriorated materials to disk a process best left to the commercial sector or should libraries attempt inhouse optical disk programs similar to current microfilming operations? How will such programs be staffed? Should regional conversion centers be considered?
- Since information on disk can be accessed from remote locations, should one or only a few libraries become national centers for information preserved in this format? If the materials stored on optical disk are not likely to be used frequently, is there still a legitimate need for multiple copies to be held by a number of libraries? How will the cost of acquiring and staffing local optical disk collections compare with that of providing remote access? Which approach will ensure the best quality of public service?

- What are the copyright implications when libraries producing the original disks send copies to other institutions?
- Since information stored on disk at remote locations can be accessed from home or office, what will be the impact on local library operations? To what extent should users be required to absorb the online cost?
- Who should be responsible for regenerating information on disks purchased from the commercial sector when replacements are no longer available? What are the proprietary rights of producers when images begin to degrade?

While many unknowns cloud the rapidly developing optical disk technology, it seems to offer great possibilities for libraries. As with many other issues in collection management and preservation, the common concerns arising from new developments in electronic media should promote continued communication and cooperative problem solving.

References

1. Ross W. Atkinson, "Selection for preservation: a materialistic approach," *Library Resources and Technical Services* 30 (1986): 341–53.

2. Roger S. Bagnall and C. Harris, "Involving scholars in preservation decisions: the case of the classicists." *Journal of Academic Librarianship* 13 (1987): 140–46.

3. Margaret S. Child, "Further thoughts on Selection for Preservation: a materialistic approach," *Library Resources and Technical Services* 30 (1986): 354–62.

4. "Conoco study sets the stage for shared collecting," *Research Libraries Group News* no. 13 (1987): 4–7.

5. John F. Dean, "Conservation and collection management," *Journal of Library Administration* 7 (1986): 129–42.

6. Patricia A. McClung, "Costs associated with preservation microfilming: results of the Research Libraries Group study," *Library Resources and Technical Services* 30 (1986): 363–74.

7. Nina J. Root, "Decision making for collection management," *Collection Management* 7 (1985): 93–101.

8. G.R. Thoma, S. Suthasinekul, F.L. Walker, J. Cookson, and M. Rashidian, "A prototype system for the electronic storage and retrieval of document images," *ACM Transactions on Office Information Systems* 3 (1985): 279–91.

9. Gay Walker, J. Greenfield, J. Fox, and J.S. Simonoff, "The Yale Survey: a large-scale study of book deterioration in the Yale University Library," *College and Research Libraries* 46 (1985): 111–32.

Information Technologies and Collection Development

by Jutta Reed-Scott

Perhaps the most striking characteristic of today's information environment is the pace of technological innovation. The phenomenal increase in computer memory capacity and speed of access, and the development of ever more powerful but less expensive computer chips, stimulate creation of expanded applications. The changing nature of automated systems requires continuous adjustment to cycles of expanding, ever-changing information systems.

More libraries have integrated, online automated systems in place. Such systems permit the use of a shared computer database for such applications as acquisitions, serials control, circulation, and public access catalogs. This results in greater processing efficiency, and allows integration of bibliographic and holdings data, on-order information and circulation records.

OPPORTUNITIES AND COSTS

One vital characteristic of the current technological environment is the rapid growth of machine-readable bibliographic records made possible by centralized bibliographic networks. These not only support shared cataloging, but also make possible rapid bibliographic access to vast but decentralized research holdings. Millions of machine-readable records have increased the visibility of collections and fostered more effective resource sharing. Not surprisingly, this has created enormous pressures on libraries to convert millions of catalog cards to machine-readable form.

Decentralized access to collections has many advantages; it also brings new challenges. The transition to integrated systems may demand re-structuring of departments, increased coordination among library units, and more staff training. As automated systems assume a larger role, increased attention is focused on the quality, completeness, currency, and maintenance of the database. This in turn may require detailed analysis of the cost of creating and maintaining records, greater use of local options in catalog maintenance, and improved quality control.

Technological advances also drive the emergence of local area networks and the capability to integrate library systems into campus- or city-wide networks. The installation of local area networks provides the potential to access library files and to transmit bibliographic information and text from the library to users' computers.[1]

Again, enhanced access to library resources is not without costs. Not only must the library commit funds to support the needed hardware and system maintenance, it must also provide substantial funds for system enhancements and data enrichments that make dial-access and effective use of information possible. The "library without walls" also poses the difficult issues of responding to users who have varying levels of searching proficiency and who only access the library from remote locations.

Technological breakthroughs shift greater computing power into the hands of end users. In the last five years there has been an immense increase in use of computers. The 1985 American Council of Learned Societies' survey of scholars underscored this fact revealing that over 50 percent of the respondents use computers for their research.[2] It is evident that the use of computers will continue to expand rapidly. Moreover, workstations will become significantly more powerful than today's

> One vital characteristic of the current technological environment is the rapid growth of machine-readable bibliographic records made possible by centralized bibliographic networks

Jutta Reed-Scott is Collection Development Specialist for the Association of Research Libraries' Office of Management Studies.

personal computers. The next generation of computers is expected to integrate voice and data, include full text retrieval, support greater use of artificial intelligence and provide yet more sophisticated workstations.[3]

Still another significant characteristic of the information environment is the computerization of information. The emergence of electronic publishing and the introduction of optical disk technology make possible mass storage of full texts and their retrieval on demand. But the new electronic formats require extensive system support. They also raise complex questions of how to pay for the information and who is to pay.

As the information environment changes and computer systems become more pervasive, the pace and scope, and the cost, of changes become more significant. For collection management, the implications of these developments center on three crucial areas: availability of more extensive management information; transformation of the nature of collections; and changing patterns of user access and information use.

COMPUTERS & COLLECTION MANAGEMENT INFORMATION

New technologies and expanded library automated systems are enabling collection development librarians to obtain management information on the cost of building collections, on the growth patterns of collections, on the dimensions of collections, and on the use of the collections. While the full impact on collection management is only beginning to emerge, it is apparent that automated systems offer many new tools and benefits.

In the area of collection building, automated acquisition systems have proved a boon to collection managers, providing them with detailed information on the growth of the collections. Acquisition systems make possible title counts of additions to the collection and allow analysis of new acquisitions by subject, language, country, and type. In addition, acquisitions systems offer a multiplicity of fiscal data and are invaluable in budget planning and administration.

Beyond library acquisition systems, information generated by vendors enables collection managers to keep track of publishing output in their fields, to monitor expenses for serials, and to forecast price increases.

Applying computers to collection assessment is another area of great import. Probably the most publicized application is the use of data from circulation systems to identify little-used or heavily used portions of the collection and to document use patterns over time.

Recognizing the limitations of use-centered collection assessments, recent efforts have focused on collection-centered approaches. One important resource is the library's machine-readable files. Computer-assisted analysis of bibliographic tapes allows determination of collection strengths and weaknesses. In recent years AMIGOS Bibliographic Council, Inc., has marketed a collection analysis service that generates report data for groups of libraries based on their bibliographic tapes. Beyond this commercially available service, several libraries have developed special programs to chart collection growth using the library's automated bibliographic files.[4]

The installation of online, public access catalogs will play an important role in understanding the composition, growth pattern, and depth of collections. At present, 50 large research libraries and more than 300 special, academic, and public libraries in both the United States and Canada have operational online catalogs. Moreover, the number of operating systems is rapidly growing. The 1986 *Automation Inventory of Research Libraries* documents that a "22 percent increase in the percentage of libraries reporting integrated online catalogs occurred between 1985 and 1986."[5]

From a collection management view, online catalogs have significant potential to provide vast information not only on the composition of the collections but also on how they are used. For example, online catalogs provide information on the collections by class number, language, date of publication, or subject. Equally important, online catalogs improve the library's ability to generate data on collection demands.

On national and regional levels, installation of computer systems is supporting a range of coordinated collection evaluation efforts. The RLG Conspectus and the North American Collections Inventory Project (NCIP) are providing a standardized collection methodology for mapping collection strengths in research libraries. The results are recorded in a special database, the RLG Conspectus On-line. Gradually, the Conspectus model has been adopted by regional groups, by the Canadian Association of Research Libraries, and even western European countries. Without the use of specialized databases for recording participant libraries' collection levels, coordinated collections assessments would be far more difficult, if not impossible.

It is clear, then, that automated systems have an immense potential to enhance collection management processes. Yet the practical problem of digesting the massive amount of data generated by these systems has not been dealt with effectively. There is a real danger of information overload because the systems' capability to generate data far outstrips the collection development managers' capability to analyze and interpret the data. Given the variety, complexity and quantity of potential data, there is a need for effective collection management information systems. These systems will become essential if collection managers are to exploit the machine-generated data for improved decision-making and effective use of collection resources.

THE NEW FORMATS

Computerization of information is transforming the nature of research collections, and of collection management. Added to traditional print materials, will be computerized bibliographic, textual, and numeric data files. Information resources of all descriptions are already available in machine-readable format. Among these are full text files such as encyclopedias, directories, journals, newspapers, court cases, and patents. Another category of online data is numeric, including U.S. Census, stock market and numerous statistical series. Still other machine-readable data include cartographic information, chemical structures, and medical references. While electronic publishing is still young, it clearly is a growth industry. Continued changes in the technology of producing information and demands for increased productivity will fuel electronic publishing, especially in the areas of science and technology information.

But these new uses and formats for information are forcing libraries and publishers to face some difficult legal and economic issues. On the legal front, questions center on copyright, ownership of electronic information, and rules of access. On the economic front, how to fund access costs is the critical problem. This is aggravated by a plethora of commercial databases and information services with varying fee structures and requirements for technological support. As the costs of access to electronic information increase, libraries will have to reallocate existing resources, seek additional funding, or recover costs.

In response to cost problems, libraries are developing different strategies and mechanisms to pay for access to electronic information. Some libraries pass a portion or even all costs to the user. Others incorporate access to electronic data into the operational budget and provide no-charge access. Still others establish a continuum from no-charge access in some cases to fee-based service

for commercial databases or extensive searches. All libraries must rethink their services and make some complex choices that will affect user access to information and library budgets.

Beyond commercial electronic publishing, increased use of computers for scholarly communication will change the concept of building collections. Because electronic texts are fluid and interactive and are changed frequently, it will be difficult to capture information. Building collections will move from a static process of acquiring library resources to a more fluid position of providing access to information. The expanding function of the library as a gateway to information will shift the emphasis from local collections to access to information not owned by the library but made available through library systems.

The impact of new data storage technologies will be equally dramatic and will further increase the complexity of our information resources. With the advent of CD-ROM the composition of collections will change further. The advantage of this new technology is high storage density coupled with microcomputer-assisted random access capabilities. Because CD-ROM disks can store between 10,000 and 20,000 pages of text, they are an attractive medium for storing full text and its retrieval on demand. Building on available computerized files, current applications of optical technology include reference works, financial sources, and medical information. Beyond applications for high-use information, the Library of Congress is investigating the potential preservation benefits of optical disk technology. Recent developments hold considerable promise for linking CD-ROM systems to online services. As noted in a recent article in *The New York Times*, this utilizes the big storage capacity of disks for historical data, but links the user to online services for up-to-date information.[6]

Again, the new technology is not without problems. The high cost of these systems may be only the most obvious serious obstacle. Incompatibility between different systems, lack of standards for database formats, and proprietary product software are major drawbacks. Despite these problems, optical disk technology will play an increasingly important role in libraries and will force them to deal with the problems. As CD-ROM continues to evolve, predictions are that digitized, full text will be an *essential* component of collections.[7]

As the scope of computerized information expands, the challenge grows to link new services to traditional library resources. This leads to some difficult questions about how to select, how to

There is a real danger of information overload because the systems' capability to generate data far outstrips the collection development managers' capability to analyze and interpret the data control, and how to integrate electronic information into the collection management process.

ESTABLISHING LINKAGES

Electronic technology makes rapid access to information possible, but it is an extremely costly selection decision. Providing the dollars to acquire the needed hardware and/or cover usage fees requires substantial reallocation. The impact on the collections budget can be enormous. The choice of whether to spend materials funds to provide access to electronic information or to acquire the information in print is complex. The critical issue is that these are frequently not substitutional costs, but substantial add-ons.

For the foreseeable future, libraries will need to acquire materials in print as well as offer online access. As user demand for electronic resources increases, a balance must be maintained between acquiring printed materials and supporting access to electronic information. Without appropriate planning, there is the danger of a shift from widely accessible, inexpensive information in traditional print sources to less accessible, costly electronic information.

How will libraries keep track of the rapidly increasing volume of information? On the one hand, there is fragmentation of information caused by new information systems, many of which cannot communicate with each other and all of which are expensive to use. On the other hand, there is the increasingly interdisciplinary nature of scholarly research, which requires access to many sources of information. For collection managers, the proliferation of information resources, the rising tide of commercial products, and the changing nature of research are making collection building and management more complex.

In the print-based environment, a major collection development responsibility is the organization and maintenance of collections. In an electronic environment, the long-term survival of information becomes "an intellectual and technological problem." Electronic formats require not only specialized delivery mechanisms but also ongoing system support. Providing access to an expanding array of information resources requires collection development librarians to have the technical knowledge to manage collections in a variety of electronic formats.

CHANGING PATTERNS

New information technologies will make fundamental changes in information access. The online catalog will change the way users gain access to information about collection. In contrast to card catalogs, online catalogs, online catalogs provide vastly enhanced access through Boolean searching capacity. The capacity to access the library files from an office, dormitory, or home will not only place information closer to users, but will accelerate user demands for electronic information.

Library users will be able to create, store, and distribute information. It is apparent that students and faculty on university campuses, and users in special libraries and public libraries, equipped with their personal computers, will demand access to the libraries' automated files. Users will not only want to download bibliographical information about specific items in the collection, but access the content itself. The more files that can be accessed, the more users want. As users' expectations for text delivery through their personal computers rise, greater demands will be placed on the library to provide electronic access to a multiplicity of information. A danger is that an unbridgeable gap will open between users' expectations and the library's ability to support ever-increasing access costs.

The confluence of many forces is transforming collection management. The challenge, as Patricia Battin noted, is "to integrate information technology into the existing information system in a way that preserves the linkages to the existing knowledge base, encourages and stimulates the productive use of new technologies, and provides coordinated gateway access to the universe of knowledge in a manner convenient and invisible to the end user."[8] Though the responses of individual libraries to that challenge can be expected to be different, at least temporarily, those responses will shape how the challenges are met as new technologies find a place in the library environment.

References

1. Carlton C. Rochell, "The Next Decade: Distributed Access to Information," *Library Journal* (February 1, 1987): 44.
2. Ronald H. Epp and JoAn S. Segal, "The ACLS Survey and Academic Library Service," *College or Research Library News* (February 1987): 63.
3. John P. Crecine, "The Next Generation of Personal Computers," *EDUCOM Bulletin* (Spring 1986): 2.
4. Evelyn Payson and Barbara Moore, "Statistical Collection Management Analysis of OCLC-MARC tape records." *Information Technology and Libraries,* 4 (3) (1985): 220–232.
5. Erik Sandberg-Diment, "Data Bases: The Best of Both Worlds," *The New York Times,* (Sunday February 8, 1987): F18.
6. *The Automation Inventory of Research Libraries,*

1986. Maxine K. Sitts, editor. (Washington, D.C., Association of Research Libraries, Office of Management Studies, Systems and Procedures Exchange Center, 1986), p.1.

7. Martin M. Cummings, *The Economics of Research Libraries* (Washington, D.C., Council on Library Resources, 1986), p. 97.

8. Patricia Battin, ''The Electronic Library—A Vision for the Future,'' *EDUCOM Bulletin* (Summer 1984): 13.

Developing Serials Collections in the 1990s

by Sara C. Heitshu and J. Travis Leach

Managing the serials portion of collection development in research libraries demands the wisdom of Solomon and the patience of Job. The difficulties presented by variations in format, title, and quality of content; bibliographic control; escalating costs; storage; and preservation, not to mention the shifting teaching and research needs of a large campus, require a combination of bibliographer/subject specialist, economist, cataloger, preservation expert, and bibliographic instructor. The interrelationships among library staff, faculty and the library administration can be tested to their outer limits when making decisions about serials.

While it may be argued that serials have always been difficult, it cannot be denied that recent events in serials publishing, pricing, cataloging, and automation have made the work of librarians far more complex than ever before. The economics of serials—including inflation and pricing— have severely affected research libraries in the past fifteen years and will continue to do so.

Efforts to solve problems of selection, processing, and control have produced an extreme range of organizational structures. At one end of the scale all serials work is performed by a dedicated staff under one manager; and at the other, serials are treated no differently from monographs and are integrated into the general work flow. However, neither of these extremes, nor the variations in between, really addresses the problems of managing serials in a research library unless communication about serials decisions in general, and individual titles in particular, reaches and is understood by all of the library staff and the library users.

Communication about a serial title from the point of selection of the title until it dies or is cancelled must be current, continual, clear and concise. Instead, information about serials usually begins and ends with the decision to add a title to the collection. While this may be an acceptable method of dealing with some library materials, it is clearly insufficient when dealing with a format defined as "a publication in any medium issued in successive parts bearing numerical or chronological designations and intended to be continued indefinitely."[1] Librarians engaged in the business of collection development in research libraries must be prepared to actively monitor serials intellectually, bibliographically, physically, and economically for as long as they continue to be part of a library's collection.

Historically, bibliographic control of serials has not been treated as a collection development issue, but in fact, it is. Collections are only of use if the materials in them can be found. Serials records are easily lost in enormous card catalogs or hidden in special lists. The difficulty of updating any form of control system is enormous; so is the problem of whether to classify or alphabetize titles, and where to shelve journals and other serial continuations.

THE CATALOGING DILEMMA

For many research libraries full cataloging of all serial titles, even the most ephemeral, was and is the norm. Others, caught in the dilemma of the cost of such cataloging versus the necessity of providing public access to their collections, have opted for serials lists of various kinds. And, it is not unusual to find major collections within a research library represented by special finding tools created for the users of specific collections. Data processing provided some relief for the production and maintenance of serials lists. Only recently

> . . . it cannot be denied that recent events in serials publishing, pricing, cataloging, and automation have made the work of librarians far more complex than ever before

Sara C. Heitshu is Assistant University Librarian for Technical Services at the University of Arizona. J. Travis Leach is Acquisitions Librarian at the University of Arizona.

have online interactive systems offered an optimal solution to the management of ever-changing serials records.

The conventions used in traditional cataloging and in serials lists have generally depended upon the cataloging practice of the time. The normal choice of entry was often the issuing body usually represented by multiple part corporate entries which required either elaborate cross references or an instinctive feel for the right order of words on the part of the user. Generations of library users are probably still automatically inverting headings such as the University of Arizona, to: Arizona, University, as they approach the card catalog.

The new *Anglo-American Cataloging Rules* attempted to remedy the situation in 1967, but the Library of Congress refused to fully adopt the rules and the era of superimposition began. Since most research libraries depend upon LC copy for cataloging and since the card catalogs, serials lists, and other bibliographic tools of these libraries had long and elaborate histories based on following LC practice, albeit with local variations, the rules had little effect on serials access. Still, new generations of serials and reference librarians thought there had to be an easier way. Title access was the cry of the seventies When the Library of Congress finally did apply AACR to headings, giving us the era of desuperimposition, a brand new code was already well on its way.

The second edition of the *Anglo-American Cataloging Rules* published in 1978 brought changes of a truly sweeping nature. Titles were most often the choice of entry, and the distinction between the hundreds of reports which a research library might hold was entirely dependent upon the selection of qualifiers. Corporate headings which had mostly escaped during the tenure of AACR now had to be flipped to conform with the new rules. Automation promised to make this easier, but few major research libraries had fully automated databases. Opening a new card catalog helped monograph catalogers, but was a nightmare for serials catalogers. It is not clear that catalog users have been well served in either case.

In addition, the full implementation of the philosophy of successive title cataloging, touted as ideally suited for the automated environment which was just around the corner, occurred in the 1970's. A title change could now create an entirely new bibliographic record to which a discreet holdings statement could be attached. A linking note led the catalog user back to the previous title. The practice of "title varies" notes was no longer acceptable. It is little wonder that public services staff were bewildered about what to tell library users about how to find serial titles.

CONSER PROJECT

The CONSER project made a national serials database more than just a serials librarian's dream. CONSER refers to a cooperative program for online serials cataloging that resides in the OCLC system. The CONSER file was built upon brief union list entries upgraded by CONSER libraries, and upon the new cataloging of these libraries, and the Library of Congress. It promised to be a tool for shared cataloging and shared resources. Standards for machine readable records and their content were a major event in the 1970's. They also heralded the resurgence of interest in serials automation. The retrospective conversion of serials records in an online environment was a real possibility, not just a dream, and bibliographic records could be linked with holdings statements and easily up-dated.

Local and federal funds were poured into conversion projects in the 1970's and early 1980's. Unfortunately, funds available were not enough for most large libraries to adequately clean up truly old bibliographic records. Cosmetic changes to headings were easily accomplished, but the piece checks necessary for recataloging each successive title change were not possible in many libraries. In spite of national standards, a national database, and a nationally accepted cataloging code, the variations in serials bibliographic control continued and seemed to multiply since many of the variations were now online for all to see.

Union lists, once simple home grown products, were the new focus of bibliographic control as the 1980's began. If a national database was possible, so were nationally based union lists. Even small libraries with no access to OCLC have become part of regional and state union listing groups. The new products possible are remarkable in both size and scope. Whether they are truly an acceptable substitute for the older, simpler lists remains to be seen.

CONTROLLING SERIALS COLLECTIONS

Despite all the changes during the '60s, '70s, and '80s bibliographic control of serial collections is still expensive, labor intensive, and may not always be effective. To provide adequate access, it is necessary to commit large amounts of high level staff time. Costs have not been lowered by automation or rule changes or national databases. It is also doubtful whether a user seeking a serial title in a major research library collection is any better off as a result of the changes.

A selector/bibliographer must strive to understand the principles underlying serials control, as well as the records in his or her library. When issues related to the identification, classification, or cataloging of serials arise, it is important to consider how national standards may apply. When problems arise over where to classify, when to analyze, or what access points to select, the selector/bibliographer ought to represent the public point of view.

Check-in

Added to the complex issues of bibliographic control is the matter of check-in. Each piece must be recorded in some manner when it is received. Manual systems abound, and some research libraries maintain holdings information in a variety of places—kardexes, shelf lists, circulation systems, and local union lists. Different staff members may be responsible for the various files and different rules and regulations may govern the form and function of the files. Associated with check-in is claiming. The integrity of a serial depends upon the receipt of all of its parts. Claiming must be precise and punctual in order to be effective. At the same time, it cannot be done by rote since all delinquent serial titles in a research collection cannot be claimed on the same rigid schedule, and not all are of equal importance. Selectors must indicate priorities for claiming, and subject specialists, particularly for geographic areas, must be consulted before months are spent claiming third world serials. Thus, the day-to-day maintenance of serials collections is also a major task. Staff may not be at the highest classification level, but they must be well trained in the vagaries of serials and understand the systems of control used in their library. The job is complex but can be boring, and high staff turn-over is not unusual. At the same time, there is a need for continuing rapport and communication between that staff and the librarian/selectors in order to ensure that efforts to maintain the integrity of the collection are suitably directed.

Automation of the check-in function holds some real hope for streamlining serials control. Systems developed in the 1970s which depended upon databases and software maintained outside of the library had significant drawbacks. In the 1980s really effective serials control systems are available either as part of an integrated package or as a separate stand-alone system. With check-in files online, random access to records is possible, check-in itself may be done with one or two key strokes and claiming becomes semi-automatic. The record file is no longer confined to one physical location, but is available through terminals in public areas. Binding information also may be come part of the system display, solving a major problem for public service staff and library users. The old excuse of "it must be at the bindery" is no longer possible.

Preservation

The preservation of a serial is another complex issue. Binding standards for serials have undergone a dramatic change in the 1980s. Awareness of preservation issues and new mechanical and chemical processes have made the classic Library Binding Institute Class A binding only one of a number of options available. In addition, pamphlet binding or other in-house binding methods, filming in-house or through a contractor, and the purchase of commercially published film or fiche copies are other options. The matter of a film product is further complicated by the continuing debate over silver halide and diazo film.[2] While the choice between film and paper print may be obvious in the case of a national newspaper or a locally produced small magazine, other cases are not always as clearcut. The selector/bibliographer must think of the use to which a title will be put, the frequency of use, and length of time it can survive in useful condition in a particular format.

Economics

The economics of serials collection development is its most complicated aspect. Traditionally, it has been beyond the control of librarians, watching passively from the sidelines as rising costs devastated their budgets, leaving less and less money to buy books, and consequently endangering the integrity of their collections.

Yearly subscriptions to periodicals, indexing services, and standing orders for other serial continuations have soared during the last 15 years. At the same time, library materials budgets have shrunk due to local, national, and world economic conditions. These events coincided with the proliferation of new serials publications, a large part of the widely experienced information explosion. Throughout the "watershed years," as James[3] calls them, of advances in serials management and control, growing concern about pricing overshadowed the considerable theoretical and technological achievements in making the information in these same publications more accessible to library users.

A glance at the three major annual periodical price indexes—A.L.A., B.H. Blackwell, and Faxon reveals the magnitude of increases. These indexes differ in the core base of titles, and in methodology but the trend they portray is the same: a sixfold increase over 15 years.[4] The causes of rapidly rising subscription prices have been studied but they still remain obscure. They do not seem to be based on costs to publishers in labor and supplies; nor can they be explained by distribution costs in transportation and postage. The price increase ratios far exceed the inflation rates recorded in the U.S. Consumer Price Index. In fact, the prices of monographs have been relatively stable over the same period of time.

Library/publisher relationships have been damaged by ignorance and misunderstanding. Publishers know little about the problems of library administration, materials budgets, and serials collection development. And librarians, even administrators and acquisitions librarians, are generally ignorant of the greater world of business for profit. How a periodical is priced seems to be known only to the publisher. However, librarians know or surmise the following:

- Publishers, having known costs and projecting the expected number of sales, can calculate a subscription price that will bring in the desired profit.
- Publishers charge what the market will bear.
- Publishers differentiate between personal and institutional (multi-reader) price: the "soak the library" syndrome. How they calculate the institutional price is unclear to librarians.
- Learned society publishers have perfected the art of exploiting the nonmember. The library may be precluded from membership as a consequence of membership restrictions, structure, services, or cost. However, the library is eligible to subscribe to the society's publications at the nonmember rate, which is, of course always several times higher than the member rate.
- Some publishers set prices based on the customer's geographical location. For example, many British publishers have a three tier pricing policy: the lowest price for customers in the United Kingdom, the highest price for U.S. customers, and a third price for the rest of the world.
- Scientific publications are more expensive and rise in price at a much greater rate than publications in the humanities and social sciences.

Regardless of how prices are calculated, it is obvious there have been excesses, to the detriment of library budgets. Librarians regard ruthless pricing policies as especially audacious since most authors from whom publishers benefit are not paid for their work. In fact, an author may even pay for the privilege of being published. A further irony is that these same scholars are almost entirely dependent on libraries as sources of information.

How much profit is fair? Are libraries subsidizing prices for individual subscribers and society members? Are U.S. libraries subsidizing foreign libraries? This last question finally goaded librarians into testing their collective influence by vociferously questioning these pricing tactics. On this side of the Atlantic it appears to be a clear case of price gouging using geographically-based dual pricing. Increases have been as much as 40 percent or more per year for subscription renewals to overseas customers, mainly U.S. and Canadian libraries.

Librarians have also accused foreign publishers of pricing based on unrealistic exchange rates. Foreign publishers justified their actions on the relative decrease in the dollar's strength and on the historical deficits they had experienced when the dollar was strong. It is interesting to note that American publishers have been using similar geographically based pricing tactics, although perhaps not to the same extent. All in all, it appears that misunderstandings of a fundamental nature exist between American libraries and publishers, foreign publishers in particular. Some progress has been made to unravel the misunderstandings and to effect a de-escalation in the dual price differential. In the meantime, this situation has profoundly affected serials collection development in U.S. libraries and has helped bring into focus the many factors outside the title selection process.

Publishers employ other strategies that cost libraries more. Smaller publishers shortchange libraries and publish fewer issues than advertised by using the tactic of "delayed" issues which ultimately become "combined" issues without a simultaneous reduction in subscription price or an extension of the paid subscription. The free issue claiming period for expected issues is commonly much shorter for expensive, commercially published titles, than for less expensive titles. Also, to obtain a replacement for a single missing issue of say, a quarterly journal, these same publishers, require the library to buy the entire volume or year, or charge as much as the yearly subscription rate for a single backissue. The latter case extends to certain microform publishers, as in the situation where a volume takes several reels to reprint. Some publishers, particularly of scientific journals, have for many years offered "supplements" and "additional volumes" to subscribers. These issues are published and priced in addition to the established subscription price and announced much later in the subscription term. The rate of occurrence in publication of these additional issues has recently accelerated.

THE COPYRIGHT DILEMMA

Other issues surround serials titles in a research environment. Copyright is one. In the past, librar-

How much profit is fair? Are libraries subsidizing prices for individual subscribers and society members? Are U.S. libraries subsidizing foreign libraries?

THE COPYRIGHT DILEMMA

Other issues surround serials titles in a research environment. Copyright is one. In the past, libraries have been responsible only for use made by library staff of copyrighted materials, and patrons have been left to be guided by their own consciences prompted by signs to remind them of the law. Recently, however, periodical publishers have been adding charges to invoices for the right to copy.

Gordon & Breach explained the sudden appearance of 10 percent additional charges on renewal invoices as the "photocopy licensing fee," to offset losses in revenue by illegal photocopying. But librarians believe the publisher is already protected under U.S. copyright law. This additional fee, coming on the heels of the British publishers' dual pricing excesses, scandalized librarians. These tactics create unanticipated additional expense to the library. Under pressure, Gordon & Breach partially rescinded the fee, but librarians can expect more extortion from journal publishers.

THE PLANNING DILEMMA

Unlike other areas of serials collection management such as cataloging, automation, indexing/abstracting, and indeed, definition of the published entity,[5] there has been little effort toward economic standardization. There is no standard for predicting library budget needs for serials. There is no standard way for allocating funds to subject areas or to other areas such as location or new study/research programs. There is no standard way of predicting periodical subscription price increases. Few standards exist as guides to format selection and purchase, that is, print vs. microform, or format of microform. There are few standards for binding, claiming, replacing missing parts, preservation and conservation, or sharing of resources between libraries to reduce the expenses for any one library.

Is Cunning Enough?

So, in order to stay afloat and not get soaked too badly, each library relies on its own intellectual resources and cunning to administer the budget. However, there is an underlying principle behind a serials budget: funds must reliably appear each year to cover renewals of the serials each library has selected. Each subscription to a serial implies a commitment by the library to a future outlay of money, space, and time. The source of the renewal funds must be reliable and relatively stable, such as state funds or the yields of large private endowments. Short term grants or donations to cover any part of the serials renewal budget are not acceptable because they may vanish with little warning.

Serials' steady drain on budgets has become critical and has brought into question the optimal allocation of the budget between serials and monographs. Currently, allocation of from 40 percent to 60 percent of the budget to serials is considered acceptable by university library administrators. Of course, the optimal allocation depends on the local serial title mix. Academic libraries supporting strong science programs may allot as much as 70 to 80 percent of the budget to serials. Early fears that serials would consume the entire budget ignored the fact that this would be in no one's best interest, including the publishers. Librarians have had to learn to make hard choices in cancelling serial titles and adding new titles.

Crystal Ball or Algebra?

Since subscription prices are rising faster than library budgets, trying to predict future renewal costs is necessary. This has been attempted in a number of ways, uncertain at best, since many factors are unknown. Of about equal use are educated guessing based on past performance, or a good crystal ball with which to contemplate inflation. However, since greater confidence and accuracy are urgently desired, a few more promising methods, have been formulated.

Mathematical analysis of trends has at last lent some credence to the "science" in library science. For example: Emery has shown the relationship of periodical price increases to times to be quadratic and that "we may therefore with confidence opt for a forecasting model for periodical subscription costs based on the concept of the geometric mean, since this is the model that provides the best trade-off between costs and benefits.[6] Clark and Williams of the Harvard Widener Library have devised a local periodical price index for titles in the humanities and social sciences and say it correlates very well with the Blackwell Index. They note that "with these results the library feels comfortable in using the linear regression method of least squares to determine the slope of the regression line of the Widener Combined Index on the Blackwell Index for the period 1971 to 1982 and to predict the Widener combined average prices for the next five years," and add that it would be ideal if the Blackwell Index appeared in time for correlation to take place.[7]

cost model study for the National Commission on the New Technological Uses of Copyrighted Works. It proposes the following:

> Many libraries are now facing reduced budgets; the rapidly increasing costs of periodical subscriptions, the new copyright law and the proposed national periodicals system have focused special attention upon periodical acquisitions and potentials for controlling or decreasing expenditures in this area.
>
> To realize these potentials, it is highly desirable to be able to estimate the costs of options associated with acquiring periodicals. This report uses a mathematical model for estimating such costs to address the following question: *Should a library own (i.e., subscribe to) or should it borrow, when needed, a specific periodical?* [8]

USING SUBSCRIPTION AGENTS

However poorly librarians have managed external matters of pricing in their communications with publishers, they have made internal matters work to their best advantage through the use of subscription agents. Approximately 95 percent of American libraries use subscription agents to help reduce staff time and money spent on serials collection development and management.

Theoretically, agencies have agreements with publishers and, as middlemen, collectively submit orders and claims for their clients in an effective, efficient, and organized manner. Cash is sent with the orders, eliminating publisher invoicing. Economies of volume reduce costs to agencies below what a library would pay for the same title. Agencies also earn revenue from short term investments of money prepaid by clients for annual subscription renewals, advertising serial titles, and the sale of software for serials control systems. The services the agent provides to the library are based on these revenues. Historically, whether an agent charged a service fee or extended a discount to the library depended on the above cost margin, competition from other agents or from the publisher, and the cost of the overall services which the library asked the agent to provide. However, since the late 1960's publishers have lowered or deleted discounts to subscription agents and service charges are the norm. This has not significantly altered library/vendor relations except to bring the agent and its performance under greater scrutiny by the library.

Libraries still find agencies highly effective in reducing overt and hidden expenses that would be incurred if the library placed each subscription directly with the publisher. Hidden expenses include cost of writing checks or purchase orders, supplies, telephone service charges, postage, up-dating publisher address files, and staff wages and time. Rigorous cost analysis of this system is difficult, but superficial observations indicate that a library may save as much as 90 percent in clerical work on ordering alone and 50-85 percent on claiming by using a subscription agent.

Some agencies can provide custom management/cost reports to their clients, or they can be accessed online thereby eliminating the cost of letters, postage, forms, and telephone calls. Agencies are also better equipped and experienced in dealing with foreign publishers in their own languages and currencies, and often save time in the process.

Although librarians have questioned the subscription agencies' service charge structures, and have suspected them of contributing to escalation of prices, agents have successfully defended their positions and seem eager to have frank and open relationships with their clients. Indeed, some agents have made efforts to help librarians pay lower prices. As the goals of library collection management change, so will the role of the vendors. They must continue their efforts to serve libraries' increasingly complex needs.

DECISIONS DECISIONS DECISIONS

Adding a serial title to a research library collection creates external and internal issues that go beyond traditional questions of content, indexing, price, paper quality, and appropriateness. The decision to buy should include a careful assessment of what type of access should be made available, frequency and urgency of claiming, retention, and physical preservation or merely content preservation. The matter does not end with these decisions. The economics must be carefully monitored year by year, while watching the quality of the title. Editors change, content and subject matter may shift for better or for worse. Teaching and research emphasis on a campus may change dramatically. The decision to cancel a particular title may come up at any time.

Just as there is no perfect formula for budget allocation to serials, there is no perfect organizational structure for optimum serial collection management. Each research library seeks ideal answers. Even if the present arrangement works, the future is very much in question.

Electronic data processing is a powerful influence dissolving old concepts of what a research library is. Electronic formats for serial index and abstracting services have already changed the role of libraries and librarians. Serials in electronic format bring new challenges, with internal control problems as yet unknown. The external factors of price and format are fluid. As we have seen with traditional serials, the decision to subscribe is only the beginning. Bibliographers, selectors, collection developers, whatever they are called, must now become collection managers whose duties are no longer confined to the selection of printed materials. New demands on the collection manager's expertise will emerge: how to provide access to information through electronic networks? what hardware/software systems are appropriate? how to balance costs for acquisition and storage of information, with convenience and confidence of access to this information?

Will the library ever stop receiving traditional paper-format pieces? Will the cost of online access make that option prohibitive for all but the grant-funded researcher, while students and less well-connected faculty continue to manually search printed sources? Striking a balance between the cost of information and access to information will be difficult. If access only is bought, who will be responsible for backfiles? How will they be accessed? Copyright becomes an even more complex issue when dealing with online access to information. Not only is it feasible to copy electronic data but also to manipulate it in a variety of ways. How will the library user know what is available or even what is an appropriate source for information sought? If traditional serials records have presented problems in the past, imagine the challenge in an electronic future. The problems of bibliographic control, preservation and economics will continue to be paramount in the electronic tomorrow just as they are today.

References

1. *Anglo-American Cataloguing Rules,* 2nd. ed., edited by Michael Gorman and Paul W. Winkler, (Chicago: American Library Association, 1978), 570.
2. See articles by Jerry Dupont and Suzanne Cates Dodson in *Library Resources and Technical Services,* 30 (January/March 1986), 79-90.
3. John R. James, "Developments in Serials: 1977." *Library Resources and Technical Services,* 22 (Summer 1978): 294–309.
4. For a fuller discussion of periodical pricing, see: Ann Okerson, Periodical Prices: a History and Discussion," *Advances in Serials Management* I (1986): 101–134.
5. See American National Standards Committee Z39, Draft Revision of Standard Z39. 1–77 "American National Standard for Periodicals: Format and Arrangement", Washington, D.C., 1983. The ANSC Z39 is now called National Information Standards Organization Z39 (NISO Z39).
6. Charles D. Emery, "Forecasting Models and the Prediction of Periodical Subscription Costs," *Serials Librarian* 9 (1985): 4–22.
7. Sally Williams and Mary E. Clark, "Using Locally and Nationally Produced Periodical Price Indexes in Budget Preparation," *Library Resources and Technical Services* 27 (1983): 345–356.
8. Vernon E. Palmour, Marcia C. Bellassin and Robert R. V. Wiederkehn, *Costs of Owning, Borrowing, and Disposing of Periodical Publications* (Arlington, Va., Center for Naval Analyses, 1977) CRC 342.

A Museum of the Book

by R. H. Super

The Modern Language Association of America recently sent a circular to all its members, beginning, "Where would *you* look if you wanted to find articles, written in Spanish, documenting speech pathology in six-year-old children?" For myself, I would have to answer "I don't know," and in the back of my mind lurk Rhett Butler's famous parting words to Scarlett O'Hara. No doubt any scrap of knowledge is preferable to complete ignorance, but creative research requires that the same mind frame the questions, recognize the answers, and perceive their relevance.

The MLA's question is all too typical of the current unthinking devotion to machinery and jargon, the approach that treats books as sources of "information," then expects someone else to pluck out that "information" and place it in a data bank. Distinguished librarians, in key positions in their profession, speak of the need to keep up with the "information explosion," and library students are trained in "Technologies for Information Management." There is, however, an equally current term that might more accurately replace "information management" in many cases; it is "trivial pursuit." More than once I have sat through meetings of research scholars being addressed by librarians intending to educate them in the use of databases, and the formula is always the same: "Suppose you want to know about. . . ." We are very grateful for the time these librarians devote to us, and warmly appreciative of the personal contact they establish with us, yet we leave such sessions bewildered or amused: nothing that has been said has any bearing on our own research, or indeed on the way we use the books in the library.

Perhaps the most important point is that the research scholar, unlike the librarian, is not looking for answers to other people's questions; for the researcher, *both* the questions and the answers grow, reciprocally, out of the research process. As I work along, I observe something that puzzles me—why did this happen in this way, I wonder? And then I turn aside to follow another path for a time, in the hope of finding the answer to that question. That the question has never occurred to anyone else in precisely the same form, or never heretofore been answered, does not diminish its significance; this may indeed turn out to be the most original and important aspect of the research. It must be remembered that no database can supply information that has not been put into it by someone, and it would be too much to expect that that someone, who is dealing with hundreds of informational problems of all kinds, will perceive the kind and form of information that I, who have spent a lifetime in a narrow field, require.

A recent writer in the *Times Literary Supplement* (E.F.D. Roberts) urges us to "be very wary of those professional colleagues who are only too ready to force on to historical and literary scholarship the relatively simple information requirements of the scientist;[1] it should be added that the true scientist also probably requires more than relatively simple information. I shudder to think what kind of research would be done by a scientist who formulated a question like the one the MLA sent to its members to generate support for its online bibliography. Librarians are constantly helping students solve problems set for them by their professors, and it is important that students develop these problem-solving skills, but the so-called "research paper" is a learning exercise; it is not research. It is learning to read the notes on the scale; it is not playing the concerto.

Roberts goes on to argue that, "whatever else it may be, a [research] library must be a Museum of the Book." As he rightly says, the term "museum" may suggest a place to take our children on a rainy day, or a building to house useless antiquities which we are reluctant to discard—even some that evolutionary wisdom did discard and which meddlesome human beings have dug out of the rocks to reconstruct as the skeleton of an allosaurus

> There is a current term that may accurately replace "information management" in many cases; it is "trivial pursuit"

R.H. Super is Professor of English, Emeritus, at the University of Michigan.

or a trachodon. But researchers in natural science know better; some of their most significant work is done by studying specimens in their museums, and scholars without access to a museum are severely handicapped. For the non-scientist the museum may be even more important: the museum of the book may catch the imagination of its users in ways that are entirely unpredictable to those who have assembled it.

My own interest has been principally in nineteenth-century British literature, and a pre-eminent characteristic of that literature—obscured by the editions in which most readers encounter it—is its inextricable intertwining with the journalism of the day. Twenty-seven (or perhaps twenty-eight) of Trollope's forty-seven novels were first published serially in periodicals, and seven more in parts issued separately at intervals (usually monthly). Nearly all the books of prose Matthew Arnold published were collections of articles that first appeared in periodicals. What difference does it make? Well, if a work is issued in installments, an author may refashion the later parts in response to criticisms of early parts. Dickens was deluged with letters urging him not to let Little Nell die (though she did die; he was too great a player on the human heartstrings to forego a death-bed). The novelists, in fact, often began serial publication of their work before the work was completed, and Thackeray, Mrs. Gaskell, Dickens, and Trollope all died during serialization of one of their unfinished works, so that we can speculate to eternity on the solution to *The Mystery of Edwin Drood*. The first time I read *Culture and Anarchy,* as an undergraduate, I was quite puzzled to understand by what clairvoyance Arnold in chapter II of his book could respond to Frederic Harrison's comment on a statement Arnold had made in his first chapter. I had no way of knowing then that the second chapter actually appeared six months after chapter I in *The Cornhill Magazine.*

Moreover, certain effects of suspense were possible with serialization. The ninth part of *Vanity Fair,* in September, 1847, closes with a description of Brussels during the battle of Waterloo, and then its very last sentence alters the focus: "No more firing was heard at Brussels—the pursuit rolled miles away. Darkness came down on the field and city: and Amelia was praying for George, who was lying on his face, dead, with a bullet through his heart." Modern readers can adjust to the shock by turning the page and reading on; the original readers (as Thackeray was of course well aware) had this sentence echoing in their minds for a full month before they could learn more.

Censorship by an editor was a threat to authors who published in magazines, but not generally to those who published in books so long as they were within the law. Both Arnold's *Literature and Dogma* and Ruskin's *Unto This Last* were stopped early in their careers by the editor of *The Cornhill Magazine;* the editor of *Good Words* paid for, but would not publish, Trollope's *Rachel Ray* because it ridiculed puritanical Christians who frowned on dancing. The censorship might be more limited and specific. In one of Trollope's novels, *Is He Popenjoy?*, the principal male character, a married man, is pursued by a woman he once courted but who is now married to another. The editor cut out the sentence in which the man reflected on "that commandment which he weekly prayed that he might be permitted to keep." Trollope was allowed to say of him that it was "so hard to be a Joseph," but the editor crossed out the shrewd observation that "the Potiphar's wife of the moment has probably had some encouragement,—and after that Joseph can hardly flee unless he be very stout indeed." Nor would the editor allow the woman to speculate with whom her husband "consoles himself," nor to say, "I hope someone is good-natured to him, poor old soul." These are not earth-shaking matters, but the essence of literary history, as of the art of literature itself, is attention to detail, and to discover these details one must turn to the original journals.

There are more important aspects to periodicals. Fully one-tenth of the pages in my edition of Matthew Arnold's *Complete Prose Works* are writings that before 1960 were available *only* in the pages of nineteenth-century periodicals. Trollope published not only novels but short stories in periodicals; only within the past few years has modern scholarship made these available to readers with no access to the original journals. And he published some two hundred articles of various lengths and on various subjects that have never been republished. Moreover the journals provide not only the texts but the contexts of these articles, Arnold's, and others; to what were they responding, and how did their contemporaries respond to them?

If, then, my own research in nineteenth-century literature requires a library that lets me browse widely in the journals of the period, my teaching requires that the same resources be available to the students I am training. They must be able to range at large, to see what the various periodicals are like, how they handle comparable subjects. This is a matter of *exploration*, not of getting answers to particular questions, nor of tracking down specific items in a bibliography. These students will have acquired knowledge of an important, if little known, aspect of literature even if they never do research in the Victorians. Those who do follow the path to research will publish significant books like the history of an important nineteenth-century publishing house, a study of the works (books and articles) of W.H. Hudson, and analytical bibliographies of articles on Trollope and Mrs. Gaskell; they will have done histories of two of the most significant journals of the era, the *Fortnightly Review* and the *Contemporary Review,* and of the magazine Trollope established and edited, the *St. Paul's Magazine.* Nor is the need for exploration confined to scholar-historians of literature; critics also must sample widely and choose for themselves. Far too many students become victims of fashion or fad when they cannot range for themselves.

Sometimes the scholar's requirements must seem very peculiar indeed. I was once a visitor for a year at another university, and was pleased to see that its library owned a complete run of the most influential weekly journal of literature, science and art in nineteenth-century England, *The Athenaeum.* And then it turned out that every volume had been bound *without* the ten or twelve pages of advertisements that were part of each issue. Why would a modern scholar want advertisements dating back a century and a half? In this case, because most ads in this journal were publishers' advertisements that give important evidence of the publishing history of books. (Fortunately sets in other libraries have preserved these pages.) Researchers' needs are unpredictable to the outsider, and often even to themselves, until they arise. There is something very naive in removing all volumes of the *Contemporary Review* earlier than 1900 from the stacks—not because they were in bad shape physically (a very good reason indeed for protecting them if that had been the case) but presumably because someone thought volumes published before 1900 were of little interest in the modern world.

Nor will such technology as the microfilm, whatever its convenience, replace the journal in its original form. A student I knew once got out the issue of the London *Times* in which Gerard Manley Hopkins read of the wreck of the steamship *Deutschland.* The newspaper article is well known to Hopkins scholars; what the student discovered, however, was that on the *opposite* page was an article that had no connection with the wreck but which contained ideas Hopkins incorporated into his very complex poem. The bound volumes of a newspaper are very cumbersome, but had the student used microfilm the discovery would never have been made because on film the two pages are not opposite one another.

A photograph of a book or manuscript will not show such vital things as watermarks: watermarks can distinguish one state of a book from another

and, since they often carry dates, watermarks can frequently be used as evidence for dating letters and manuscripts. One very skilled editor and teacher recently remarked, in a description of his research, that the scholar who relies entirely on photographs is at the mercy of a photographer who has no notion of the needs of the scholar; may not realize the importance of postmarks on the *back* (as well as the face) of an envelope, may fail to note a Postscript on the back of a leaf; indeed the folds of the letter paper may testify in which one of several envelopes that letter was originally sent. He went a step further by showing a photograph of a letter on which ink had been spilt; nothing could be made of it. But techniques of infra-red lighting when used with the original letter recovered most of the text.

We are told that an increasingly significant function of the information manager is to classify and define data. But classification cannot be done independently of the *use* to which the data will be put. I recently heard a distinguished biologist present a new view of Darwinism that validated his evolutionary theory only by looking at aspects of development *other than* the usual classification by species. The library catalog used to be relatively easy to use; a knowledge of the alphabet was the only prerequisite. Recently, in a genuine spirit of helpfulness, a tendency has grown to break up the alphabetical sequence into an infinity of subject headings. The seeker after a book must match with the classifier. The more recently acquired books about Thackeray are filed under thirteen subject-headings, each with its own alphabetical sequence. Among these are "criticism," "language," and "technique." What distinction the classifier was making I cannot imagine; I know only that I am obliged to leaf over many more cards than formerly if I am to find the book I want. Instead of a help, classification has become a hindrance, and will be even worse when I must wait for each entry to appear in slow sequence on a video screen. The former simplicity has given way to cumbersome complexity, and, what is worse, gives an impression of absoluteness which can cramp the student as it already seems to have cramped the Library of Congress classifier.

The library is to humanists what the laboratory is to scientists, with the important distinction that humanists share their libraries with far more people than scientists their laboratories. Such sharing has the tremendous advantage of widening the resources available to humanist researchers: under the same roof I can use books on a very wide range of subjects, all of them necessary to my work. But whereas scientists can design and manage their own laboratories to meet their needs, the library is necessarily managed by people other than the researchers. Decisions are made that will change the pattern both of my research and of the way in which I instruct my students. I have spoken of the importance I attach to an intimate acquaintance with periodicals in my field, and to the ability to browse freely among them. In the midst of a recent semester I discovered that whole shelves full of these periodicals had been removed to another location where they were inaccessible to students, and a seminar was destroyed. At the same time I was systematically going through the nineteenth-century volumes of the *Bookseller,* a monthly journal of the British publishing trade, for trade gossip, advertisements, and announcements, in the course of assembling data on the publication history of Trollope's novels. One day I went to the stacks to continue my search and found the shelves empty.

The pressure of space is sending more and more of these journals away to storage facilities where browsing is impossible, and students are often denied access. I have no solution to this problem. There are too many humanists on the campus for library management to keep track of the activities of each one. And administratively, it is easier to remove a hundred feet of a single title than to gain the same space by removing separate monographs. Nor can a manager distinguish which books to remove except by irrelevant criteria such as date of publication or frequency of circulation. As new books are acquired space must be made for them, and often such space is not available close to the campus library building, so that older books must be removed. But by no means all the shortage is caused by the pressure of new books. Within the

past decade shelving in the main building of my own university library has been very markedly reduced to make room for library offices and, now, for machines. They are the wave of the future.

A historian colleague of mine who shares my sentiments tells me he regards a collection of books as the embodiment of Edmund Burke's idea of a contract between the living, the dead, and those generations as yet unborn. It fulfills that contract, and its community of scholarship has the same kind of extension through time. The humanist can only regret the sad lack of humility which reduces all knowledge to "information"—information in the sense of our current technology—and one must hope that in our conceit we do not altogether destroy our past.

Like paleontologists humanists needs their museums—museums of books; like physicists and chemists need their laboratories, we need shelves through which to browse. A university's reputation often depends on its humanist scholars, and they and their work must be preserved. If this sounds a bit mercenary, let me say that there is real joy in making discoveries for one's self, more joy in seeing one's students make them, and the library in which discoveries can be made will be the real preserver of the past by giving it meaning to new generations as they use that past to build a future.

References

1. *E.F.D. Roberts, "The British Library: directions and locations," Times Literary Supplement,* Feb. 3, 1984, p. 123.

Alexandria Revisited: Another Look at Space and Growth

by Sheila Dowd

A little over a decade ago, a major library problem was formulated in arresting and witty terms. The growth of library collections, and the consequent pressure for growth of library buildings, was the subject of a conference of the Associated Colleges of the Midwest; and the conference, which proved to be seminal to the next decade of managerial thought, proclaimed that we were "Touching Bottom in the Bottomless Pit."[1] So we bade *Farewell to Alexandria*[2]—that is, to the purported dream of all libraries, infinite expansion. In the same period the University Grants Committee of Great Britain was studying the same question. They, with the authority of the governmental voice, mandated a fixed size for British university libraries—a "no growth" policy.[3] In the ensuring years, "no growth" has been a policy for some libraries, an uncomfortable physical fact for many others.

In justice to the "bottomless pit" conferees it must be acknowledged that their focus was not on research libraries, but on academic as well as other libraries. A number of speakers acknowledged the different functions of different kinds of libraries. Even so draconian an advocate of no growth as Richard Trueswell concedes that "if the primary function of a library is to support research into the farthest depths of obscurity (which may be important), then the question of size becomes irrelevant."[4] Nonetheless, the thinking reflected in *Farewell to Alexandria,* and the University Grants Committee report, has had substantial influence on research library planning and politics in the ensuing decade. It is the growth requirements of such institutions that are considered here.

The containment philosophy of *Farewell to Alexandria* embodies several assumptions regarding libraries and scholarship. One is that knowledge is outdated at the same rate it is published, and the library can therefore be self-renewing like a perennial crop. Another is that it is possible to accurately predict the prospective use of publications. And a third is that scholars seek the record of knowledge in isolated pieces, rather than in relationship to other elements of recorded knowledge. These assumptions must be examined. The question of how big a library should be can only be answered after we have determined what the library is for, and how its users work.

THE PURPOSE OF THE RESEARCH LIBRARY

What is a research library for? It is, and has been throughout its long history, a social institution created to collect the record of human knowledge, to organize and make it available for use, and to conserve it for future use. The functions of the true research library are inescapably both archival and service-oriented. The *Twenty-Sixth Annual Report* of the Council on Library Resources asserts, "The archival and the information service roles of libraries, which are quite different, are not yet fully defined for our time, and the best means to meet the responsibilities inherent in each are not yet worked out."[5] The phrase "which are quite different" perpetuates a fallacy that has impeded the defintion of these roles and the identification of means to fulfill them.

Proponents of no growth typically ignore the archival function of the libraries under discussion, assigning such responsibility to a very limited number of institutions. Daniel Gore, for example, suggests that little-used publications might be housed in six storage libraries nationally—two each for the humanities, the social sciences, and

Sheila Dowd was Assistant University Librarian for Collection Development at the University of California, Berkley, until her recent retirement.

A respectful attention to users' own assessment of their working methods, and their consequent needs, must be the basis of research library planning the sciences.[6] The previously mentioned Report of the British University Grants Committee (commonly called the Atkinson Report) recommends reliance on the British Library Lending Division as the archival repository for all British university libraries except Oxford and Cambridge. *The University of California Libraries: A Plan for Development, 1978–1988*[7] prescribes two compact shelving repositories to house lesser-used materials stored by more than 30 academic libraries in the state, with further relegation of inactive materials from the storage facilities to the Center for Research Libraries. In each of these proposals the archival role is not perceived as central to the active functioning of the research library.

For many libraries the dichotomy between archival and service roles is valid. A great many libraries simply do not have an archival role in any long-term sense. Their information service role can dictate their collecting and retention, and permit them to maintain an equilibrium. Their equilibrium will, of course, depend on the availability of archival collections somewhere else. As David A. Kronick has written, "The no-growth library cannot function effectively except in relation to growth libraries, which makes the problem a collective rather than an individual problem."[8] For the research library the dichotomy does not exist. The strength of the library as a research resource rests as much on its success in collecting, maintaining and organizing the human record as it does on the provision of services to link scholars to that record. The archival functions of collecting and preserving are intrinsic parts of the research library's service. It is in this perspective that we must re-examine the assumptions that knowledge replaces itself; that collection use is highly predictable; and that the user is typically seeking an isolated piece of recorded knowledge.

THE LIFESPAN OF KNOWLEDGE

The Great Library of Alexandria was organized in the reign of Ptolemy Philadelphus (285–246 BC). That ruler launched an aggressive acquisitions program in every port of Greece and Asia to secure the most valuable works, regardless of cost. His successor, Ptolemy Euergetes, is said to have taken an even more aggressive course, ordering that all books brought into Egypt by foreigners be seized for the Library. It is fair to assume that the Ptolemies aimed at what the RLG/NCIP Conspectus terms "Comprehensive Level" collections: collections "in which a library endeavors, as far as is reasonably possible, to include all significant works of recorded knowledge . . . the aim, if not the

achievement, is exhaustiveness."[9] The limitations of book production in the third century BC might make the comprehensive library a conceivable, if manic, goal for a Ptolemy. No modern library can even dream such a dream; the Conspectus notes that the comprehensive level collection is "for a necessarily defined and limited field. . . . This level of collecting intensity is one that maintains a 'special collection.'"[10] The degree to which research libraries can be said to have Alexandrian goals resides in the commitment to preserve and make accessible as much as possible of the human record.

The holdings of the great Library of Alexandria are estimated at between 400,000 and 800,000 papyrus rolls (each roll containing substantially fewer words than a modern volume). The collections of the Library of Congress number over 20,000,000 volumes, although in very few areas does it define its collections as "comprehensive." The difference in size gives some measure of the extension of human knowledge, and the technology for recording that knowledge, in the intervening twenty-three centuries. But the papyri of ancient Egypt continue to be counted among the greatest treasures of a few fortunate modern libraries—not inert treasures, but living documents which permit scholars to study such questions as the role of women or commercial practices in that ancient society. So too the records of the Inquisition allow LeRoy-Ladurie to bring into vivid relief the life of a medieval village; the data tapes of the 1960 and 1970 U.S. censuses remain relevant as bases for later and increasingly significant demographic and social analyses of U.S. population. Information resources are not regularly superseded. Discoveries build on earlier explorations, and the record of human knowledge is cumulative and constantly growing. The Atkinson Report set the goal of the "self-renewing library," a research library in which new acquistions are to a considerable extent offset by withdrawals. A British librarian, confronting the impact of this policy, cogently asserted that "one cannot improve a research library by what amounts to a long-term replacement of its stock."[11]

THE SCHOLAR'S USE OF LIBRARIES

Recorded knowledge, then, has a long life. The reasons for its longevity are embedded in how scholars work; and they belie assumptions that use is highly predictable, or that scholars typically seek specific or isolated pieces of recorded knowledge. An English librarian, David Paisey, has stated the problem well:

The precise mechanics of the process of humanities research in libraries are little understood and studied by planners, a fundamental gap in their equipment. This can lead to inadequate library structures based on interlending strategies, in which scholars are seen as requiring single books, or single items of information, rather than related (often remotely related) groups of texts whose composition and configuration cannot be foreseen, with the back-up of limitless secondary material, current and non-current, any or all of which may be cross-disciplinary: in other words, the universal reference library. In the U.K. it is the dominance of current science and technology which tends to blind planners to the existence of more complex models than that of literature use in those areas: though the structure of humanities research is equally experimental, its materials are texts.[12]

The humanities scholar (and, to a greater degree than is usually conceded, the social scientist and the occasional scientist, too) works from source to source, not in linear sequence, but in an ever-widening ring of references, citations, leads and discoveries. The statistical evidence of use studies ranging from Fussler and Simon's 1961 study[13] through the celebrated surveys of Trueswell,[14] Kent,[15] and others seem to offer unarguable evidence that, in the words of John Boll,[16] "... works that have not circulated for a number of years in an academic library are even less likely to circulate in the future." Numerous studies followed Fussler and Simon's conclusion that unrecorded use (sometimes called shelf browsing or in-house use) closely parallels circulation, leading Boll to assert, "It seems safe to treat circulation figures for a category of works as proportional to, and therefore indicative of, total use figures for that category...."[17] The data for this last conclusion have failed to persuade innumerable scholars, and innumerable librarians who serve them. The resistance has been, on the whole, less formulaic and statistical than the arguments for close relationship between circulation and in-house use. This is probably because the use being studied is not measurable; circulation is regularly recorded, but to record "unrecorded" use is to add an extra process for the library, and, more importantly, for the user who is presumably scanning shelves partly to avoid completing time-consuming records.

At least one library, the University of California at Riverside, is compiling a substantial body of statistics to compare in-house use and circulation. Preliminary analysis of the data suggests that the expected correlation does not apply for a significant portion of the collection.[18] The faculty of the University of Pittsburgh responded to the Kent study in writing.[19] However, the weight of the argument that a wider body of materials is used in

shelf consultation rests soundly on the testimony of scholars: most librarians serving the humanities have heard scholars say that they use shelf-consultation and browsing as a regular element in their research strategies. Analysts, theorists, and others committed to blazing trails through administrative thickets tend to discount personal testimony and to assume that such information is uncritical hearsay. Like any other data, perceptions born of experience must be examined and tested; but for questions about scholars' working methods, they themselves are surely the most reliable source. Certainly the belief, widely held among humanists and humanities librarians, that scholars consult a wide and unpredictable mass of materials is substantiated by the source acknowledgments in publications.

Use studies are often arbitrary in allowing what constitutes meaningful on-site use. Fussler and Simon, for example, attempt to differentiate between "valuable" and "not valuable" browsing in their analysis of user-survey response. They dismiss the shelf browsing of a known item, a work that could have been called for by messenger, as without value in the terms of their investigation, adding parenthetically, "It is possible, of course, that there is a higher inertia threshold for calling for a book by messenger than there is for looking at a book in the stacks, but we shall not consider that of importance."[20] It is doubtful that many scholars in the humanities would endorse that judgment. Research commonly leads the humanist from a known body of literature to other works uncovered through a web of citations, through the structure provided by a classed collection, or through an increasingly complex apparatus of subject access tools. The mass of material to be examined is immense, since, for most topics, relevancy cannot be predicated on publication date. To scan and reject as unnecessary to the work at hand is one indispensable element of the search. And to find inertia setting in at the prospect of filling out the two hundredth call slip is a human failing which may have regrettable consequences for the quality of research.

A respectful attention to users' own assessment of their working methods, and their consequent needs, must be the basis of research library planning. Those needs will include the identification of seemingly endless pieces of information, to be sure; but they will go beyond this to the rationally organized collection which relates kindred things, and so promotes the distillation of orderly knowledge out of random information. For productive research in an age of overwhelming resources, there will be need for extensive, readily available research materials, with few obstacles between the scholar and the publication. In short, there must be organized research collections close to the scholar, which will, inexorably, grow.

OPTIONS FOR CONTAINING GROWTH

If we accept the premise that growth is inherent in a vital research collection, we can apply ourselves to managing growth for the most cost-effective support of research. As Richard Dougherty notes in an editorial, there's nothing wrong with self-sufficiency as a goal for a library, except that nobody can afford it.[21] Or, in Kronick's words, "The question, How large a library should I have? can be answered by another question, How large a library can you afford?"[22] No library can, of course, be sufficient in itself for all the complex needs of an academic research community; but each must try to establish the collection growth necessary to support the discipline it serves, and must then realistically consider the physical space required to organize those materials for effective scholarly use.

Strategies currently being employed by libraries to contain physical expansion include:

- Storage of materials at a remote facility owned by the library or by a cooperating group of libraries
- Reduction of text size by miniaturization (microform or electronic data storage)
- Reduction of storage space requirements by compact shelving
- Purchase avoidance or de-selection based on reliance on the collections of another library or a consortium of libraries.

All research libraries are employing some of these approaches, and many are using all, in applications suitable to various elements of their collections.

STORAGE

Storage encompasses a variety of provisions, ranging from the transfer of materials to a nearby annex, to the deposit of materials in a distant regional or national facility. It usually (though not invariably) includes a shelf arrangement that makes optimum use of space at the expense of classed array. Obvioulsy, the accessibility of the storage facility and the recovery-time for wanted items are important factors in determining how much of its collections the research library can store without seriously damaging the scholarly enterprise. But even with optimum turnaround time, the integrity of the collection as an interrelated and organized whole—what Paisey calls "related (often remotely related) groups of texts whose composition and configuration cannot be foreseen . . ."—will suffer in proportion as it is fragmented.

In discussions of space needs, no topic is more vigorously contested than browsing. To arrange a large collection in browsable order is to sacrifice potential economies of space and of maintenance staffing, and library planners are justified in challenging the importance of such an arrangement. John Boll offers the following summary of the arguments against shelf browsing:

> Five categories of reasons make shelf browsing a less than reliable subject access device for serious research:
> 1. The items may have been temporarily removed from their shelf location without the browser's knowing it;
> 2. The items may never have been classed in the logical location in which the shelf search occurs;
> 3. There may actually be several logical browsing locations for a concept, only one of which is likely to be known to the browser;
> 4. Many classes, and even minute subdivisions of classes, exist in large libraries that are too large for browsers to search effectively;
> 5. No library resources can replicate the total available resources on any subject as well as a group of bibliographical tools can.[23]

The five arguments are all true; and yet the conclusion that browsing is therefore unimportant to "serious research" is not supported by the real behavior of serious researchers. They do browse. They stand at the shelf to scan other works in the subject area of a known item; to compare editions of a work and select the most useful (or perhaps just the least messy copy); to verify citations; to find useful titles without a time-consuming bibliographic search; to be led by the rational scheme of a classification system from one concept to another in a period of idea-gestation. They are fully aware of the five caveats listed above, and they do not rely totally or even principally on browsing; but for most humanities scholars direct access to an organized collection is an important element in effective working patterns.

Most large libraries face inexorable space pressures forcing them to move books out of central locations. Boll concludes, "The time has arrived for every academic library of 1.5 million volumes or over to shelve from 33% to 50% of its collection compactly, in-house and/or in a separate storage facility, with sized shelving."[24] The University of California, Berkeley, library fulfills this thesis. It reached capacity in its Main Library stack in the mid-sixties, and by the mid-eighties stored over half its humanities, social sciences, and general or interdisciplinary collections at a facility several miles off campus. User dissatisfaction with the fragmentation of the collections is increasingly persistent and widespread. Many scholars assert that research is very difficult as storage cuts more and more deeply into the immediately accessible and browsable collections. At the same time the library pays added costs for selecting materials for storage and in helping users identify and retrieve items. The capital costs of building are clear and quickly comprehended. Less widely understood are the continuing operational costs of managing a growing collection that must perpetually be weeded for remote storage, serviced in multiple locations, and efficiently retrieved. Furthermore, the serious hidden costs to scholarship have not been analyzed. The Berkeley experience suggests that there is a point of diminishing returns in the fragmentation of collections at which costs to scholar-users outweigh the institutional economies sought.

Using low-cost real estate for book storage may be deemed a necessity, but it is a solution which incurs major problems. More thoughtful study of the costs and benefits of remote storage is needed before the space needs of the living research library are creatively met.

MINIATURIZATION

Dramatically reducing the size of text for storage, and enlarging it again when needed, is an alluring idea for anyone wrestling with space and size problems. Miniaturization technologies are changing rapidly, with techniques for electronic storage of information. They are still in their infancy, at present largely a matter of reformatting paper on microfilm or microfiche. But experience with microform tells us that miniaturization of collections must be applied selectively, with judgment, and understanding of the scholarly process.

Microform is welcomed by scholars when it gives immediate access to works previously available only from a distant location—a manuscript from another library, a document from a foreign archive, etc. It is accepted with equanimity when it permits great masses of data to be brought together for ready consultation, as in the *American Statistics Index;* or when it allows easy scanning of previously cumbersome formats, such as newspapers. It is somewhat grudgingly tolerated as the only available means to preserve crumbling paper copies. User acceptance of microform plunges for works to be read in their entirety, or for long runs of journals which they like to browse. Portability and legibility make the printed book or journal not merely a pleasing but a very practical object. It is idle for planners to dismiss this subjective value,

as they dismiss the importance of browsing, simply because it gets in the way of proposed economies.

As electronically stored information becomes more affordable, more widely accessible, and more assured of long archival life, it will be an important element in containing research libraries' growth. Compact disk storage shares some of the inconvenience of film, but omnipresent computer terminals make "portability"—or, more properly, distributability—of electronic information much greater, as does the relatively easy transfer to paper on demand. However, much more study is needed before assuming that the contents of research libraries can be transferred to disk. The quality and durabiltiy of reformatted information must be considered as well as the costs of republishing on demand for every reader.

Miniaturization poses problems similar to storage; it removes the physical text from accessible, browsable array. For works to be read as a whole, the arbitrary separation of materials lessens the value of the research collection.

COMPACT SHELVING

Perhaps the most promising development for growth containment is the increasing use of mobile shelving which permits compaction of stack aisles while maintaining collections in classed array. Many libraries are using such shelving now for selected parts of their collections. The Library of Congress made extensive use of compact shelving on the lower floor of its Madison Building, for a collection which is of course closed to the public.

The University of Illinois, Urbana, Library has made bold use of compact shelving. The great Illinois collection, numbering more than 7,000,000 volumes, is housed entirely on the Urbana campus, much of it in a central building planned for systematic stack additions. The sixth such addition, erected in 1983, is entirely consecrated to compact shelving, and houses 2,000,000 volumes.[25] The stacks are open to a substantial part of the campus community. To achieve maximum shelving capacity, Illinois embraced what might be considered the outer limits of possible compaction, compressing several aisles of 45-foot ranges in each compact block. Despite the obvious inconveniences inherent in obstructing immediate access to so many books at one time, staff members have reported generally positive user attitudes toward the new addition. This user acceptance may be attributable in part to the excellent lighting, climate control, and general attractiveness of the new addition; it is also undoubtedly due to the faculty's enlightened understanding of the trade-

The Berkeley experience suggests that there is a point of diminishing returns in the fragmentation of collections at which costs to scholars-users outweigh institutional economies

69

offs between compact shelving and other space economies.

Probably no research librarian should contemplate the institution's long-term future without giving careful consideration to compact shelving for some part of the collection. The irritations of delayed shelf-access and interrupted browsing will certainly exist; but the advantages of maintaining collections on-site and in browsable array will probably outweigh them in the minds of most regular library users.

COOPERATIVE RELIANCE

The service questions raised by excessive dependence on remote storage are applicable to over-reliance on interlibrary cooperation, too. David Paisey's comments on the process of humanities research, quoted earlier, are taken from his review of Bernhard Fabian's *Buch, Bibliothek und geisteswissenschaftliche Forschung: zu Probleme der Literaturversorgung in der Bundesrepublik Deutschland*.[26] Professor Fabian examines the "dogmatization" of interlibrary lending in Germany, where there has been heavy and institutionalized reliance on interdependence of collections since before World War I. He "sees the growth in interlending figures, not as a vindication of the interlending system, but as an index of the failure of individual libaries. Nor is the burden of interlending equalized, for it is seen to overload the larger libraries and reduce their usefulness to readers on the spot."[27] Professor Fabian is no enemy of interinstitutional cooperation; and most American scholars, too, have learned to value highly the many cooperative agreements libraries have evolved to expand the resources available to them. Again, it is a question of the degree to which a library can rely on borrowing to relieve its space and budgetary problems; and also of the point at which the costs (to library and users) of borrowing exceed the benefits. If there has been a "dogmatization" of interlibrary reliance in Germany, one might suggest that there has been a romanticization in some American library circles.

To the realist, the first and most obvious benefit of library cooperative programs is the extension of resources available to scholars. But reliance on a peer institution for materials the library could not afford to acquire in the first place is not a response to space pressures. Can libraries really save space by relying on other collections, or by not purchasing specific desired titles?

The sense of a collection as an orderly and cumulative whole, a totality more valuable than its individual parts, certainly limits the degree to which it can be weeded on the basis of coopera-

tive reliance. It is (fortunately) a rare research librarian and a rare scholar who would discard useful and relevant publications for space reasons only. But other considerations will probably give increasing impetus to cooperative collection pruning. The preservation of brittle and fragile research collections will require a financial investment beyond any resources now visible. In setting priorities for preservation, libraries will have to work together.

Purchase avoidance seems to promise more help to the book budget than to restraint of growth. The most cost-effective form is probably selective, coordinated acquisition of very costly publications—major microform sets, limited facsimile editions, etc. The space impact of such items is minimal. However, serials collecting agreements can offer substantial long-term benefits for both the acquisitions and the space budgets. Purchase avoidance on the basis of a cooperative agreement has the greatest potential when the cooperating institutions are relatively close neighbors. If a scholar can choose between two accessible and browsable collections the program will have more user acceptance than item-specific borrowing from remote collections.

INFORMATION VS. KNOWLEDGE

Daniel Boorstin has noted that knowledge is orderly and cumulative, while information is random and miscellaneous.[28] The research library is a house of knowledge, a place where the human record is cumulated and maintained in orderly, usable condition for the continuing growth of knowledge. Berkeley English professor George Starr, in a memo to campus administrators, once defined the library in terms that deserve wider distribution:

"a . . . definition of what libraries *are*: not solely or primarily repositories of bits of information, to be stored, retrieved, and delivered on demand, but places where work-in-progress can encounter work achieved. I don't deny that it's one function of a university library to answer telephone queries as to the year in which Columbus discovered America; I do deny that this should serve as the model or norm of what a university library is all about. . . . Without waxing unduly mystical or phenomenological, I think one can claim that a university library ought to be a space *within* which writing meets and absorbs the written, thinking finds and appropriates the thought, seeing perceives and reenvisions the already 'seen,' and so on. No doubt this can and will be translated into 'browsing capability' and 'seating accommodation' as the objects of my humanistic idolatry. . . .''

A mathematician, in a recent discussion, remarked that complete reliance on bibliographic access, even computerized, in lieu of ready physical access to closed collections drives scholarship into increasingly narrow focus. The student does not get the sense of a bibliographic universe that comes from browsing in a great collection; and the faculty scholar loses an important stimulus to explore ideas in ever-widening circles of thought, tending to concentrate more and more on a narrowly defined area of study. He added that intensely specialized scholars are needed, but that minds with breadth, capable of formulating and investigating linking concepts, are also essential to a healthy scholarly community.

The library planner caught between scholars' need, and the budgetary implications of collection growth, is apt to dismiss the reality of the needs, since it is impossible to be similarly cavalier about costs, if the manager is to survive in the institutional bureaucracy. As a result, efforts to achieve realistic cost and growth containment have moved libraries farther—and sometimes very far—from serving their users effectively. Where this is true, librarians must not play Dr. Pangloss, brightly refusing to recognize problems which do not yield to ready solutions.

The rhetoric of "Alexandria" and "the bottomless pit" suggests that a prudent, practical manager should accept the thesis that the library will devour its parent institution unless abruptly checked. Whether libraries in fact grow more rapidly than total campus building complexes, or than the laboratory complexes within a campus, is a legitimate question, and the answer on most campuses would probably put the Alexandrian terror in perspective.

Standing up for the library's mission and the scholar's library needs is hard and often thankless work. The university library director who uses a coping strategy, prioritizing the library's needs to fit available resources, may win acceptance from university administrators more readily than the director who does a sober, comprehensive needs analysis, documents the costs, and strongly advocates the necessary level of support.

Allocation of inadequate resources among competing areas seems to be the essence of university administration. Libraries represent a substantial element in the institutional budget, and it is understandable that the reflex response of most campus administrators will be to mandate that their costs be severely contained. Faced with the heady challenge of maintaining the house of knowledge, and helping work-in-progress encounter work achieved, in an environment of scarcity, the librarian must look for every legitimate economy and real effi-

ciency possible. Having done that, he or she must be prepared to analyze remaining needs, develop plans for addressing them, justify costs—and then fight well and hard. The fight will involve skillful lobbying and education of the campus community to the issues and impacts. The goal will be to build solid support throughout the campus community for this institution which is so often termed the heart of the university, and so rarely treated as such. Library problems are real, and solutions costly; the fight will necessarily be a continuing one. Persistence and courage are the first requirements of the librarian-advocate. Elegiac farewells and problem-avoidance behavior must give way to commitment to maintain the vitality of the research library as an essential element in the processes of scholarship.

The time has come to embrace again the Alexandrian goal of great, growing research libraries—even, in the coordinated aggregate, comprehensive ones; and to bring twentieth century knowledge, techniques, and resources together to create and maintain them. The New Alexandrian Library will be built by librarians who are politically astute, who understand economic issues, who accept a responsibility to be realistic, persistent advocates—and who are infused with an understanding of the nature of scholarship and its needs.

References

1. Associated Colleges of the Midwest Conference on Space, Growth, and Performance Problems of Academic Libraries, Chicago, April 17–18, 1975.
2. Daniel Gore, ed. *Farewell to Alexandria: Solutions to Space, Growth, and Performance Problems of Libraries.* Westport, Conn.: Greenwood Press, 1975.
3. Great Britain. University Grants Committee. *Capital Provision for University Libraries: Report of a Working Party.* London: HMSO, 1976.
4. Richard W. Trueswell. "Growing Libraries: Who Needs Them? A Statistical Basis for the No-Growth Collection." In *Farewell to Alexandria,* p. 72.
5. Council on Library Resources. *Twenty-sixth Annual Report 1982.* Washington, D.C.: CLR, 1982, p. 9.
6. Gore, op. cit., p. 178.
7. *The University of California Libraries: A Plan for Development, 1978–1988.* [Berkeley]: Office of the Executive Director of Universitywide Library Planning, July 1977.
8. David A. Kronick. "Goodbye to Farewells—Resource Sharing and Cost Sharing." *Journal of Academic Librarianship* 8:3 (July 1982): 133.
9. *RLG Collection Development Manual,* 2nd. ed. Stanford, Ca: The Research Libraries Group, 1981, p. 2–2.
10. Ibid.
11. Norman Higham. "The State of the Argument:

> The time has come to embrace again the Alexandrian goal of great, growing research libraries . . . and to bring twentieth century resources together to create and maintain them

United Kingdom." In *Steady-State, Zero Growth and the Academic Library.* London: Clive Bingley, 1978, p. 40.

12. David Paisey. review of *Buch, Bibliothek und geisteswisssenschaftliche Forschung . . .,* by Bernhard Fabian. *The Library,* Sixth Series, 6:3 (Sept. 1984): 299.

13. Herman H. Fussler and Julian L. Simon. *Patterns in the Use of Books in Large Research Libraries.* [Chicago]: The University of Chicago Library, 1961.

14. Trueswell, op. cit.

15. Allen Kent and others. *The Use of Library Materials.* New York: Marcel Dekker, Inc., 1979.

16. John J. Boll. "Shelf Browsing, Open Access and Storage Capacity in Research Libraries." University of Illinois Graduate School of Library and Information Science, *Occasional Papers* 169 (June 1985): 17.

17. Ibid, pp. 17–18.

18. In-House Use Study, University of California, Riverside. Conducted by researchers Peter Briscoe, Nancy Koller, and Jeff Selth. Funded by Librarian's Association of the University of California. Study in progress; publication planned.

19. University of Pittsburgh. The Senate Library Committee. *Report on the Study of Library Use at Pitt by Professor Allen Kent, et al. (A Pittsburgh Reply).* July 1979.

20. Fussler and Simon, op. cit., p. 194.

21. Richard M. Dougherty. "What's Wrong with Self-Sufficiency?" *Journal of Academic Librarianship* 5:4 (Sept. 1979): 187.

22. Kronick, op. cit., p. 133.

23. Boll, op. cit., p. 24.

24. Ibid., p. 29.

25. Martin H. Collier. "The Sixth Stack Addition; the University of Illinois Tops Off its Storage Capacity with a High Density, Mobile Shelving Storage Facility." *Library Journal, 107:21 (Dec. 1, 1982): 2235–7.*

26. *Bernhard Fabian. Buch, Bibliothek und geisteswissenschaftliche Forschung: Zu Problemen der Literaturversorgung und der Literaturproduktion in der Bundesrepublik Deutschland.* Schriftenreihe der Stiftung Volkswagenwerk, Bd. 24. Göttingen: Vandenhoeck & Ruprecht, 1983.

27. Paisey, op. cit., p. 299.

28. Daniel J. Boorstin. *Gresham's Law: Knowledge or Information?* Washington, D.C.: Library of Congress, 1980.

Index